THE
STORY
OF
GANDHI

By Rajkumari Shanker

Children's Book Trust, New Delhi

I recognize no God except the God that is to be found in the hearts of the dumb millions... And I worship the God that is Truth... through the service of these millions.

Mahatma Gandhi

Photographs courtesy: National Gandhi Museum, Rajghat, New Delhi

Text typeset in 13/17 pt. Bookman Old Style

© by CBT 1969
Reprinted 1971, 1974, 1977, 1980, 1982, 1984, 1985, 1987, 1988, 1989, 1992, 1993, 1995, 1996, 1997, 1999, 2000, 2001, 2002, 2003, 2004 (twice), 2005, 2007, 2008, 2010, 2011.
Revised edition 2012
Reprinted 2012, 2014.

ISBN 81-7011-064-5

Published by Children's Book Trust, Nehru House, 4 Bahadur Shah Zafar Marg, New Delhi-110002 and printed at its Indraprastha Press. Ph: 23316970-74 Fax: 23721090 e-mail: cbtnd@cbtnd.com Website: www.childrensbooktrust.com

NEHRU ON GANDHI

...And then Gandhi came...He did not descend from the top; he seemed to emerge from the millions of India, speaking their language and incessantly drawing attention to them and their appalling condition. Get off the backs of these peasants and workers, he told us, all you who live by their exploitation; get rid of the system that produces this poverty and misery. Political freedom took new shape then and acquired a new content. Much that he said we only partially accepted or sometimes did not accept at all. But all this was secondary. The essence of his teaching was fearlessness and truth, and action allied to these, always keeping the welfare of the masses in view. The greatest gift for an individual or a nation, so we had been told in our ancient books, was *abhaya* (fearlessness), not merely bodily courage but the absence of fear from the mind. Janaka and Yajnavalkya had said, at the dawn of our history, that it was the function of the leaders of a people to make them fearless. But the dominant impulse in India under British rule was that of fear—pervasive, oppressing, strangling fear; fear of the army, the police, the widespread secret service; fear of the official class; fear of laws meant to suppress and of prison; fear of the landlord's agent; fear of the money-lender; fear of unemployment and starvation, which were always on the threshold. It was against this all-pervading fear that Gandhi's quiet and determined voice was raised: Be not afraid. Was it so simple as all that? Not quite. And yet fear builds its phantoms which are more fearsome than reality itself, and reality, when calmly analysed and its consequences willingly accepted, loses much of its terror.

So, suddenly, as it were, that black pall of fear was lifted from the people's shoulders, not wholly of course, but to an amazing degree...

Jawaharlal Nehru
The Discovery of India

1

In a small, white-washed house in Porbandar, on the coast of Kathiawad in western India, Mohandas Gandhi was born on October 2, 1869. His parents were Karamchand Gandhi and Putlibai. He was small and dark, and looked no different from the millions of other children born in India. Yet this was no ordinary child. He was to fight and overcome a great empire and, without taking to arms, set his country free. He was to be called the Mahatma, the Great Soul. Having led his people to freedom, he was to lay down his life for their sake.

Porbandar is an old seaport, overlooked by the distant Barda Hills. Even in ancient days ships from far-off lands went there to trade. It was the ancestral home of the Gandhis. Mohandas' grandfather and father were famous for their ability and for their upright character.

His grandfather, Uttamchand Gandhi, who belonged to a humble family of merchants, became the Dewan of Porbandar. He was succeeded by his son, Karamchand Gandhi, popularly known as Kaba Gandhi. Karamchand Gandhi had very little formal education, but his knowledge

5

and experience made him a good administrator. He was brave and generous. He had, however, one flaw—a bad temper.

Putlibai, Karamchand Gandhi's wife, was deeply religious. Every day she worshipped at the temple. She was a lovable and strong-willed woman, widely respected for her wisdom and good sense. People often sought her advice on various matters.

Mohandas was the youngest of the six children of Karamchand Gandhi. He was the favourite child of the family and was called Moniya by his fond parents and their friends. Moniya adored his mother. He loved his father too, but he was a little afraid of him.

As a child, Moniya seldom liked to stay at home. He would go home for his meals and then run away again to play outside. If one of his brothers teased him or playfully pulled

his ears, he would run home to complain to his mother.

"Why didn't you hit him?" she would ask.

"How can you teach me to hit people, mother? Why should I hit my brother? Why should I hit anyone?" would be Moniya's prompt reply.

His mother wondered where her little son got such ideas from.

Moniya was just seven

The entrance to the house at Rajkot

6

years old when his father left Porbandar to become the Dewan of Rajkot. Moniya missed Porbandar, and he missed the blue sea and the ships in the harbour.

At Rajkot he was sent to a primary school. He was shy and did not mix easily with the other children. Every morning he went to school on time, and ran back home as soon as the school was over. His books were his sole companions and he spent all his free time alone reading.

He had one friend, however, a boy named Uka. Uka was a sweeper boy and an untouchable. One day Moniya was given some sweets. He ran at once to Uka to share them with him.

"Don't come near me, little master," said Uka.

"Why not?" asked Moniya, greatly surprised. "Why can't I come near you?"

"I am an untouchable, master," Uka replied.

Moniya took hold of Uka's hands and filled them with sweets.

His mother saw this from a window and she ordered Moniya to come in at once.

"Don't you know that a high-caste Hindu should never touch an untouchable?" she asked sternly.

"But why not, mother?" asked Moniya.

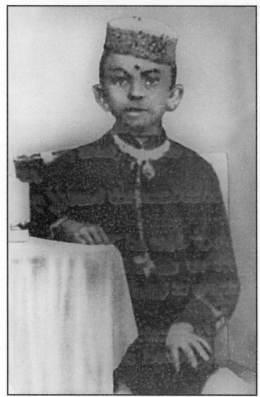

Moniya at the age of seven

"Our Hindu custom forbids it," she said.

"I don't agree with you, mother. I find nothing wrong in touching Uka. He is not different from me, is he?"

His mother had no answer. She angrily told him to go and have a bath and say his prayers.

Karamchand Gandhi loved all his sons, but he was especially fond of Moniya. He often said to him: "You must go to high school and college and take up a profession."

Moniya worked hard and did his lessons carefully. But he did not like learning by heart and was therefore weak in Sanskrit. He liked Geometry the best because it involved reasoning.

Once Moniya happened to read the story of Shravana Kumar. Shravana Kumar's parents were old and blind and he always carried them with him in two baskets slung on a yoke. Moniya was deeply touched by Shravana Kumar's devotion to his old parents. "I must be like Shravana Kumar," he resolved.

At about this time he also saw a play about Harishchandra, a king who was famous for his love of truth.

Mohandas at the age of fourteen

8

"Why shouldn't we all be truthful like Harishchandra?" he constantly asked himself.

Mohandas was only thirteen when he was told that he was soon to be married. His parents had already chosen his bride. She lived in Porbandar and her name was Kasturbai. She and Mohandas were about the same age.

The wedding day approached. Mohandas was dressed in new clothes. Everyone was gaily dressed and the house was decked with flowers and banana leaves. The bridegroom, accompanied by the wedding party, left for Porbandar.

In the bride's home it was a day of great celebration. There was singing and dancing and music. At the auspicious hour the bridegroom and party arrived.

Kasturbai, dressed in red and wearing elegant jewellery, was shy but attractive. Amidst great rejoicing, Mohandas was married to Kasturbai.

The celebrations lasted a whole week and then the bride left her home in Porbandar and went with her husband to Rajkot.

Kasturbai was a pretty and lively girl. Mohandas and she often played together. Sometimes Mohandas tried to teach his young wife but she could never concentrate on books, though she was quick to learn the household work.

One day Mohandas met Sheik Mehtab, a friend of his elder brother. Sheik was tall and strong but had a bad reputation. Mohandas knew this, yet he was much impressed by him because of his physique. Sheik was a meat-eater and he often told Mohandas that if he ate meat he would also grow tall and strong.

During those days, a reform movement to bring change in the orthodox ways of life was going strong. Mohandas

His father, Karamchand Gandhi

himself had heard that many well-to-do people had started eating meat. So he also started eating meat. Initially, he did not like the taste of meat but after some time he started relishing meat curry.

Whenever he had a meat meal outside, Mohandas had to give his mother some excuse for not eating his dinner. He knew that his parents would not forgive him if they knew he had eaten meat. He was not against eating meat then, but he was against telling a lie to his mother. This feeling was gnawing at his heart and finally he decided not to touch meat again.

Mohandas had also taken to smoking in the company of his brother, his friend Sheik Mehtab, and another relative. He had to pilfer small amounts of money from here and there to buy cigarettes.

One day, in order to pay off a debt which his brother had

incurred, Mohandas stole a piece of gold. Stealing was a great sin. He knew that he had committed a grave crime. He resolved never to steal again in his whole life. He wrote down a confession of his misdeed and handed the paper to his ailing father.

Karamchand Gandhi read the confession. He tore up the paper without saying a word. The bits of paper fell to the floor. He sank back on his bed with a sigh. Mohandas left the room, tears streaming down his face.

From that day, Mohandas loved his father more and more. Every day he hurried home from school to wait on him. His father's condition grew worse and at length he died. The house was filled with sorrow.

Mohandas was only sixteen when his father passed away.

2

After passing his high school examination, Mohandas joined the Samaldas Arts College at Bhawnagar. As he did not find the classes interesting, he returned home after the first term.

There a big surprise awaited him. His eldest brother and a family friend suggested that Mohandas should go to England to study and become a barrister. Mohandas was thrilled. Here was a chance for him to see the world.

But his mother did not like the idea of his going to England. She did not want her youngest son to stay away from her. There was also the problem of money. Moreover, she feared that Mohandas would lose his caste if he crossed the ocean. The family friend assured her that there would be no such difficulty and everything would be all right. But his mother was still opposed to the idea.

"I know many reasons why it is dangerous for a Hindu to leave India," she explained to him. "You will have to eat meat. They drink wine there and you will be tempted to follow their ways. Then you might fall into bad company, and there are many other temptations which may spoil you."

"No, mother," said Mohandas, "I am no longer a child. I can look after myself."

He pleaded with her to allow him to go.

Putlibai at last gave in and allowed him to go to England. But before that he vowed never to eat meat and drink alcohol, and never to indulge in any activity that might cast a slur on his family name and honour.

Mohandas was sorrowful when he left Rajkot for Bombay, because he had to leave behind his mother, his wife and his son who was only a few months old.

With his elder brother, Laxmidas Gandhi, 1886

On September 4, 1888, Mohandas left Bombay (now Mumbai) for England. He wore a black suit, a white shirt with a stiff collar and a necktie. Thus dressed, he stood on the deck as the ship slowly steamed out of the harbour. He was sad, but he was also excited.

Mohandas never forgot his first morning on board. He felt most uncomfortable. The stiff collar pinched him.

It was quite a job to knot his tie properly. The tight, short coat also made him ill at ease. He thought that Indian dress was much more comfortable. Yet a glance in the mirror made him feel proud of himself. He thought he looked very impressive.

Mohandas was shy. He rarely left his cabin. He even ate his food there alone. He was not sure of all those unknown dishes served on the ship. He thought they might contain meat. He did not wish to break his vow to his mother, so he lived mainly on the sweets he had taken with him.

3

On landing at Southampton he looked around. He saw that all the people were in dark clothes, wearing bowler hats and carrying overcoats flung over their arms. Mohandas was embarrassed to find that he was the only one wearing white flannels.

In London he stayed at first at the Victoria Hotel. Dr. P.J. Mehta, a friend of the Gandhi family, was the first to meet him. Mohandas was impressed with Dr. Mehta's silk top hat. Out of curiosity, he passed his hand over it and disturbed the pile of the silk. Dr. Mehta then gave him his first lesson in European manners.

"Do not touch other people's things," he said. "Do not ask questions as we do in India when we meet someone for the first time. Do not talk loudly. Never address people as 'sir' whilst speaking to them, as we do in India. Only servants and subordinates address their masters in that way."

Young Gandhi found everything around him strange. He was homesick. He almost starved until he discovered a vegetarian restaurant. Struggling to learn western manners and customs, he rented a suite of rooms. He bought well-tailored clothes and a top hat. He spent a lot of time before the mirror, parting his straight hair and fixing his tie. He took lessons in dancing, but soon gave it up as he had no sense of rhythm. He tried his hand at playing the violin, but failed. He took lessons in French and elocution, but felt sleepy in the class.

His attempt to be an Englishman lasted about three months. Then he gave up the idea. He converted himself into a serious student.

"I have changed my way of life," he told a friend. "All this foolishness has now come to an end. I am living in one room and cooking my own food. Hereafter I shall devote all my time to study."

His meals were simple. He avoided expenditure on transport and went on foot everywhere in London. He started to keep an account of every penny that he spent.

Mohandas joined the London Vegetarian Society and soon found himself in its executive council. He wrote articles for the magazine *Vegetarian.*

The bar examination did not require much study and Gandhi had ample time to spare. Oxford or Cambridge was out of the question because it meant a long course and much expense.

He, therefore, decided to appear for the London matriculation examination. It meant hard work, but he liked to work hard. He passed in French, English and chemistry but failed in Latin. He tried again, and this time passed in Latin, too. Meanwhile, he progressed in his study of law; and in November 1888 was admitted to the Inner Temple.

It was the tradition of the Inns of Court, a law organisation for the students, to dine together at least six times each

As a law student in London

year. The first time Gandhi dined with his fellow students, he felt shy and nervous. He was sure that the boys would make fun of him for refusing meat and wine.

When wine was offered, he said, "No, thank you."

The boy sitting next to him said, "I say, Gandhi, don't you really want your share? You pay for it, you know!"

When Gandhi replied that he never touched wine, the boy shouted to his friends, "By Jove, fellows, we are in luck to have this chap sitting with us. That gives us an extra half bottle."

"You can have my share of roast, too," Gandhi told them, looking quite content with his bread, boiled potatoes, and cabbage. He was pleasantly surprised to find that his queer habits did not make him unpopular. The next time he went for the dinner, he had a pile of law books with him. He was taking the books to his room to study.

"Gandhi," said a student, "you are not really going through this stuff, are you?" Saying this, he snatched up one of the fat volumes. "Look, you chaps," he cried, "he is actually reading Roman Law in Latin!"

The students laughed. One of them said, "Let me tell you, Gandhi, I passed the last examination in Roman Law by studying from the guide for two weeks. Why do you slave at it like this?"

Gandhi explained to his friends that he worked hard because of his sheer interest in the subject, and that he wanted to acquire knowledge for its own sake.

After a short trip to France, he prepared for the final law examination. The results were soon declared. He had passed with high marks. On June 10, 1891, he was called to the bar. He was admitted as a barrister and the next day was formally enrolled in the High Court. The following day, June 12, he sailed for India.

Gandhi's three-year stay in England was eventful. Those were the days of great intellectual activity, and there was tolerance for every school of thought. The country as a whole was a living university. As Gandhi sailed for home on the s.s. ASSAM, he felt that, next to India, he would rather live in England than in any other place in the world.

4

As his ship steamed into Bombay harbour, Gandhi saw his brother waiting at the quayside. He ran down the gangway to meet him. As they exchanged greetings, Mohandas noticed that his brother looked sad.

"You have bad news for me?" he asked.

"Yes," his brother replied with tears in his eyes. "We did not want to disturb you during your examinations. Our dear mother...she died a few weeks back."

Mohandas was shocked. His mother had meant so much to him. He had come back to tell her that he had kept the promises he had made before he went abroad, but now she was no more. What a sad homecoming!

At Rajkot, he set up practice as a barrister. Soon, however, he was disgusted with the greed and pettiness that he found among the lawyers. Gandhi realized that it was difficult for the poor and the humble to get justice from the courts of law. He was not happy with his life at Rajkot and he longed to get away.

It was then that an offer came to him, to go to South Africa on behalf of Dada Abdulla & Co., an Indian firm

As a barrister in Johannesburg, 1900

which owned big business concerns there. The company had filed a suit against another firm for $4000. They wanted Gandhi to take up the case because he spoke English well and knew English Law. In addition to arguing their case, they wanted him to handle the firm's correspondence in English. His services were required for one year and the company promised to pay him a handsome fee and first-class return fare.

The opportunity to see a new country and new people excited Gandhi and he accepted the offer.

It was painful for him to be parted from Kasturbai again so soon, but he was determined to go. In April 1893 he left Bombay for South Africa.

5

It was a long journey from India to South Africa. Gandhi reached the port of Natal towards the end of May 1893. The first thing he noticed was that the Indians there were treated with little respect. Within a week of his arrival in Durban, he visited the court with Abdulla Seth of Dada Abdulla & Co.

No sooner had he sat down than the magistrate pointed his plump finger at him.

"You must remove your turban," he said sternly.

Gandhi was surprised. He looked around and saw several Muslims and Parsees wearing turbans. He could not understand why he was singled out to be rebuked.

"Sir," he replied, "I see no reason why I should remove my turban. I refuse to do so."

"Will you remove it or not?" the magistrate roared.

At this Gandhi left the court.

Abdulla ran after him into the corridor and caught his arm.

"You don't understand," he said, "I will explain why these white-skinned people behave like this."

Abdulla continued, "They consider Indians inferior and address them as 'coolie' or 'sami'. Parsees and Muslims are permitted to wear turbans as their dress is thought to be of religious significance."

Gandhi's dark eyes flashed with anger.

"The magistrate insulted me," he said. "Any such rule is an insult to a free man. I shall write at once to the Durban press to protest against such insulting rules."

And Gandhi did write. The letter was published and it received unexpected publicity. However, some papers described Gandhi as an 'unwelcome visitor'.

After a week in Durban, he left for Pretoria to attend to the case for which he had been engaged. With a first-class ticket he boarded the train. At the next stop an Englishman got into his compartment.

He looked at Gandhi with contempt, called the conductor, and said, "Take this coolie out and put him in the place where he belongs. I will not travel with a coloured man."

"Yes, sir," said the conductor.

He then turned to Gandhi. "Hey, sami," he said, "come along with me to the next compartment."

"No, I will not," said Gandhi calmly. "I have bought a first-class ticket and I have every right to be here."

A constable was called in who pushed Gandhi out of the train, bag and baggage. The train steamed away leaving him on the platform. Gandhi spent the night shivering in the dark waiting room.

Gandhi took this experience to heart and resolved that day that whatever the cost might be, he would fight all such injustices. He sent a note of protest to the General Manager of the railways but the official justified the conduct of his men.

Further trouble was in store for Gandhi on his journey to Pretoria. He had to travel by stage-coach from Charlestown to Johannesburg. Though he had a first-class ticket, the conductor would not allow him to sit inside the coach.

"You barrister coolie!" he sneered, "you can't sit inside with the white passengers. Ticket or no ticket, sit outside on the coach-box. That is my usual place, but I will give it to you and take your seat inside."

Gandhi was enraged at this insult. With a heavy heart he climbed up to the seat behind the driver. He was in no mood for a fight just then.

When the stage-coach stopped to change horses, the conductor came up to Gandhi again.

"Hey, sami, you sit below. I want to smoke up here," he said. And he spread a dirty sack on the step below for Gandhi to sit on.

Gandhi flared up at this. "I had a first-class ticket which entitled me to sit inside," he said, "and you made me sit here, now you want me to sit at your feet! No, I will not do so."

"You will have to," yelled the conductor. He began to punch Gandhi and tried to drag him down. Gandhi resisted. He held on to the rail, but another blow nearly knocked him down.

Some of the passengers in the coach began to shout.

"Stop that! Leave him alone, conductor," they cried.

"He is in the right. Let him come and sit here with us."

The conductor was forced to leave him alone.

Gandhi reached Johannesburg the next night, shaken by the incidents on the way. He had the address of a Muslim merchant's house there, but as it was rather late at night he took a cab to the Grand National Hotel.

The hotel manager took a good look at Gandhi and

said, "I am sorry, there is no room vacant tonight."

Gandhi knew that he was being denied a room only because of his dark skin. Now there was no alternative but to go to the merchant's house, so he went there to spend the night.

The next day he bought a first-class ticket and continued his journey by train to Pretoria.

The only other passenger in the compartment was a well-dressed Englishman. As Gandhi entered, the Englishman looked up from his newspaper, nodded to the newcomer, and continued reading. A little later, the conductor came in. Gandhi quickly showed him his ticket.

"Your ticket does not matter, sami," growled the conductor. "Go to the third class at once."

Before Gandhi could reply, the Englishman flung down his paper and glared at the conductor.

"What do you mean by harassing this gentleman?" he said vehemently. "His ticket gives him a right to be here."

Turning to Gandhi he said, "Make yourself comfortable just where you are."

Thanking him warmly, Gandhi settled down with a book.

It was late in the evening when the train pulled into Pretoria. There was nobody to meet Gandhi at the station, so he had to spend the night in a hotel.

The next day a friend moved Gandhi to a house where he lived as a lodger. There he began his study of the Abdulla law suit. Even while he was engaged in it, he found time to call a meeting of the Indians in Pretoria.

This he did with the help of Tyeb Haji Khan Muhammad, an influential Indian merchant. Only a handful of Indians attended it. It was the first time that Gandhi had addressed a meeting.

"There is too much division among us," he said. "Why should we be kept apart by differences in birth, family, caste and religion? Let us form a league representing every group and keep the government informed of our difficulties and our needs."

The audience listened to him with great interest. It was decided to hold regular meetings of all the Indians in Pretoria.

Meanwhile, Gandhi was entrusted with the task of translating into English all the correspondence exchanged between Dada Abdulla & Co. and the rival party. After studying all the facts, Gandhi was convinced that his clients' claim was just. He knew, however, that if the case was taken to court it would drag on for a long time, so he called together representatives of both the parties.

"Why don't you choose a good man, whom you both trust, to arbitrate between you?" he said.

The representatives listened to him with great attention. They were astonished at this new idea he put forward. This young man was not the kind of lawyer they were familiar with, but they appreciated his stand and agreed to his suggestion.

An arbitrator was appointed, and he gave his decision in favour of Gandhi's clients, Dada Abdulla & Co.

Although they had won, Gandhi persuaded his clients to be lenient with their opponent. They agreed not to demand the money due to them all at once, but to accept payment in easy instalments spread over a long period. Both parties were happy over the settlement.

Gandhi's first success as a lawyer was not a crushing victory over an opponent, but the triumph of good sense and humanity.

In the Orange Free State, Indians had been deprived of all their rights by a law enacted in 1888. They could stay there only if they did menial work. The traders there were sent away with nominal compensation.

Under a law passed in 1886, the Indians who wanted to live in the Transvaal were forced to pay an annual poll-tax of £3 per head. They were not allowed to possess land except in locations set apart for them. They had no franchise. If they wanted to go out of their houses after 9 p.m., they had to carry a permit with them. They were not allowed to use certain highways at all.

Gandhi felt humiliated at the way Indians were treated there. He thought it was his duty to defend their rights and remove their grievances.

He often went out for an evening walk with an English friend, Coates, and he rarely reached home before 10 p.m. He had obtained a letter from the State Attorney allowing him to be out of doors at any time without police interference.

One evening Gandhi was alone, walking at his usual brisk pace, when he was suddenly attacked and knocked down. He was injured. He struggled to his feet to face a police constable.

"That will teach you to obey the law," shouted the policeman. "No Indian has the right to walk past the President's house. Didn't you know that?" And the policeman kicked him.

"Gandhi, are you hurt?" asked a familiar, friendly voice.

It was Coates. He happened to be passing that way when he saw Gandhi being attacked.

Coates gave a warning to the policeman.

"This man is my friend and a distinguished lawyer," he

said. "If he makes a complaint against you, I shall be his witness."

Then he turned to his friend and said, "I am very sorry, Gandhi, that you have been so rudely assaulted."

"You need not be sorry," said Gandhi. "How is the poor man to know? All coloured people are the same to him. I have made it a rule not to go to court in respect of any personal grievance."

"Just like you," said Coates, who was still very angry at the policeman's behaviour.

Coates turned again to the policeman and said, "You could have told him politely what the regulations are instead of knocking him down."

"Never mind," said Gandhi. "I have already forgiven him."

Now that the Abdulla case had been settled, Gandhi thought there was no need for him to stay on in South Africa. Towards the end of 1893 he went back to Durban to book his passage to India. Abdulla arranged a farewell party in his honour.

While going through the newspapers that day, Gandhi was surprised to read that a bill (Franchise Bill) was pending before the Natal Legislative Assembly which would deprive Indians of their right to elect members to the Assembly. Here too they would be disfranchised. He brought this to the notice of the people gathered there for the party.

"What do we understand about such matters?" Abdulla Seth said. "We only understand things that affect our trade."

"This bill, if it passes into law, will make Indians extremely unhappy," Gandhi said gravely. "It is the first nail in our coffin. It strikes at the very root of our self-respect."

The Indians now realized what was at stake but they were unable to decide what to do. They requested Gandhi to postpone his departure and help them. He agreed to stay on for another month and organize resistance to the new bill.

Late that night the Indians held a meeting in Abdulla Seth's house under the presidentship of Haji Tyeb Khan Muhammad, the most influential Indian merchant there. They resolved to oppose the Franchise Bill with all their strength.

Telegrams were sent to the Speaker of the Assembly and the Premier of Natal requesting them to postpone further discussion on the bill. The Speaker promptly replied that the discussion would be put off for two days.

The Natal Indians then drew up a petition to the Legislative Assembly pleading against the bill. This was followed up by another petition to Lord Ripon, the then Secretary of State for the Colonies. This was signed by more than ten thousand Indians. Copies of the petition were circulated in South Africa, England and India. There was much sympathy for the Natal Indians' plight, but the campaign had started too late to stop the bill becoming a law.

However, the campaign did do some good. For the first time, the people of India came to know of the conditions in Natal. An even more important result was the new spirit that now awakened the Indians in South Africa.

The Natal Indians pressed Gandhi to stay on for some more time to guide them. Gandhi told them that he was prepared to prolong his stay if the Indian community would provide him with sufficient legal work. They gladly agreed to do this. Twenty merchants turned over all their legal business to him.

When Gandhi applied for enrolment as an attorney to

argue cases in court the entire bar, composed of white lawyers, strongly opposed him. However, the Supreme Court of Natal overruled the objection and he was allowed to practise.

Soon Gandhi became one of the busiest lawyers in Durban; but to him law was a subordinate occupation. His main interest was his public work. He felt that merely sending in petitions and protests would not help the Indians much. A sustained agitation was necessary.

So he proposed the formation of a permanent organization to safeguard the interests of Indians. A meeting was called to discuss this matter. The spacious hall in Dada Abdulla's house was packed to capacity. It was there, on that occasion, that the Natal Indian Congress was formed.

In 1894 the Natal Government sought to impose an annual poll-tax on the indentured Indians. These were labourers who had been recruited from India on a five-year contract, but on starvation wages. Under the contract they could not leave their employer. They were treated practically as slaves.

These men had been taken to South Africa to help the white colonizers in agricultural work. The Indians did more than what had been expected of them. They worked hard, purchased land and started cultivating their own fields. Their enterprise did not end there. They soon built houses and raised themselves far above the status of labourers. The white people did not like this. They wanted the Indian workers to return to India at the end of the contract period. To make things much harder for them, the government now imposed an annual poll-tax of £25.

The Natal Indian Congress started a strong agitation against this. Later, at the intervention of Lord Elgin, the then Viceroy of India, the tax was reduced to £3. Still Gandhi considered it an atrocious tax, unknown anywhere else in the world. The Natal Indian Congress continued its agitation but it was 20 years before the poll-tax was finally withdrawn.

Gandhi spent three years in South Africa. He was now a well-known figure. Everyone recognized his frock-coat and turban. And his practice was well-established. He realized that he was in for a long stay. He knew that the people there wanted him with them, so in 1896 he asked their permission to go home and bring his wife and children to South Africa. Besides, a visit to India would be useful in gaining more support for the Indians in South Africa. He had arranged his work so well that he could look forward to six months' leave.

6

In the middle of 1896 Gandhi sailed for India, and after 24 days landed at Calcutta (now Kolkata). From there he went to Rajkot. It was a happy family reunion when Kasturbai welcomed him with their two sons.

But the plight of the Indians in South Africa was so much on his mind that he could not be content to enjoy domestic bliss in peace. He, therefore, launched a campaign to acquaint the people of India with the real condition of the Indians in South Africa.

He met the editors of influential newspapers and important Indian leaders, including Lokamanya Bal Gangadhar Tilak, the hero of Maharashtra, and Gopal Krishna Gokhale who, like Gandhi, was already famous at the age of 27.

Wherever Gandhi went, he tried to make the people aware of the lot of their compatriots in South Africa. Many newspapers published his views and strongly supported his case. Summaries of these newspaper reports and comments reached South Africa long before Gandhi returned there.

Meanwhile, plague broke out in Bombay and threatened to spread to neighbouring areas. In Rajkot Gandhi volunteered to join a group who tried to educate the people about the need for sanitation and other measures to prevent the spread of the disease.

At the end of November, however, Gandhi received an urgent message from Natal asking him to return immediately. There were some developments which required his presence there. So Gandhi set sail for South Africa once more, taking with him Kasturbai and their two sons and also the only son of his widowed sister.

7

The Europeans in South Africa heard about Gandhi's return. They had also heard about his propaganda in India against the Natal whites. Meetings were held to discuss how to deal with him when he came back.

In the meantime, there were rumours that Gandhi was coming back with two shiploads of Indians to settle down there. It was true that some Indians were going to Natal and that they were in two ships, but he had nothing to do with them.

Gandhi's ship cast anchor off Durban on December 18. The passengers were not allowed to land before a thorough medical examination had been conducted, for they had arrived from Bombay where there was plague. The ship was held in quarantine for five days.

The whites in Durban had been agitating for the repatriation of Gandhi and other Indians, and this agitation further delayed the landing. Gandhi was accused of having incited anti-European sentiments in India. At last, after a delay of 23 days, the ship was permitted to enter the harbour.

However, a message reached Gandhi advising him not to land with the others but to wait until evening, as there was an angry mob of whites at the dock.

Kasturbai and the children were sent to the house of Gandhi's Parsee friend, Rustomji. Later, accompanied by Mr. Laughton, the legal adviser of Dada Abdulla & Co., Gandhi went ashore.

In Johannesburg, 1900

The scene looked peaceful, but some youths recognized him and shouted, "Look, there goes Gandhi!"

Soon there was a rush and much shouting. As Gandhi and his friends proceeded, the crowd began to swell until it was impossible to go any further.

All of sudden, Laughton was pushed aside and the mob set upon Gandhi. They pelted him with stones, sticks, bricks and rotten eggs. Someone snatched away his turban, others kicked him until the frail figure collapsed. He clung to the railing of a house. The fury of the whites was unabated and they continued to beat him and kick him.

"Stop, you cowards!" cried a feminine voice. "Stop attacking him!"

It was the wife of the Superintendent of Police. She came up and opened her parasol and held it between Gandhi and the crowd. This checked the mob. Soon the police arrived and the crowd was dispersed.

Gandhi was offered shelter in the police station, but he declined the offer.

"They are sure to quieten down when they realize their mistake," he said.

Escorted by the police, he reached Rustomji's house where a doctor attended to his injuries.

Later in the evening, the whites surrounded the house. "We must have Gandhi," angry voices demanded. The mob was getting more and more threatening. "Give us Gandhi or we will burn down the house," they shouted.

Gandhi knew that they might carry out their threat. To save his friend's house, he slipped out in disguise, eluding the crowd.

Two days later, a message came from London. Joseph Chamberlain, the then Secretary of State for the Colonies, asked the Natal Government to prosecute every man guilty of attacking Gandhi. The Natal Government expressed their regret to Gandhi for the incident and assured him that the assailants would be punished. When Gandhi was called upon to identify the offenders, however, he would not do so.

"I do not want to prosecute anyone," he told the Natal Government. "I do not hold the assailants to blame. They were misled by false reports about me and I am sure when the truth becomes known, they will be sorry for their conduct."

Gandhi's statement suddenly changed the atmosphere in Durban. The press declared Gandhi innocent and condemned his assailants. The Durban incident raised Gandhi's prestige and won more sympathy abroad for the Indians in South Africa.

As the struggle in South Africa continued, a change was coming over Gandhi. He had begun with a life of ease and comfort, but this was short-lived. As he became more and more involved in public activities, his way of life became simpler. He started cutting down his expenses. He took to washing and ironing his own clothes, and he did it so badly at first that the other lawyers laughed at him. But soon he became quite an expert at this and his collars were no less stiff and shiny than theirs.

Gandhi once went to an English barber in Pretoria. The barber insolently refused to cut a "black" man's hair. Gandhi at once bought a pair of clippers and cut his own hair. He succeeded more or less in cutting the front part but spoilt the back. He looked very funny and his friends in the court laughed at him.

"What's wrong with your hair, Gandhi? Have rats been gnawing at it?" they asked.

"No," said Gandhi proudly, "I have cut my hair myself."

Then Gandhi tried changes in his food. He started taking uncooked food. He believed that if a man lived on fresh fruits and nuts he could master his passions and acquire spiritual strength. He made many experiments with his diet. He even came to the conclusion that fasting increased one's willpower.

While he was thus experimenting with himself, the Boer

With the Indian Ambulance Corps during the Boer War, 1899
(Gandhi sitting in the second row fourth from right)

war broke out. The Boers were South Africans of Dutch origin. They were fighting the British.

Neither of these two white nations had treated the Indians well. Gandhi did not want to support either of them, but his loyalty to the British made him organize an Indian Ambulance corps to help them. To his puzzled followers he said, "India can achieve complete emancipation only through development within the British Empire. Therefore, we must help the British."

The British won the war and the Indian Ambulance Corps was disbanded. The newspapers in England praised the services rendered by the Indians. The relations between the Indians and the Europeans had now become more cordial and the Indians believed that their grievances would soon be removed.

It was now 1901, six years after Gandhi had brought his

family to Durban. Now he felt that his future activity lay not in South Africa but in India. Also, friends in India were pressing him to return home. When he announced his decision to his co-workers, however, they again pressed him to stay on.

After much discussion they agreed to let him go, but only on condition that he would come back to South Africa if the Indians there needed his help. He agreed to this. There were farewell meetings and presentations of gifts.

The gifts were so many and so valuable that Gandhi felt he should not accept them. He wanted to give them back to the people who had presented them, but they would not allow him to do so. He then prepared a trust deed and all the gifts were deposited with a bank to be used for the welfare of the Indian community.

8

On his arrival in India in 1901, Gandhi went on a tour of the country. The annual meeting of the Indian National Congress was being held in Calcutta under the presidentship of Dinshaw Wacha. Gandhi attended the session. It was his first contact with the Congress which he was to lead so gloriously in the future.

The Indian National Congress was the only organization which gave the people of India a chance to express their political views. It was an influential body, as many important Indians were members, but its decisions had little affect on the government.

At the Calcutta session in 1901 Gandhi had an opportunity to meet Congress leaders like Sir Pherozeshah Mehta, Lokamanya Bal Gangadhar Tilak, Gopal Krishna Gokhale and others.

He was not impressed with the way the Congress was functioning. He noticed a lack of unity among the delegates. Moreover, while they spoke English and affected the style of westerners in their dress and talk, they did not seem to bother about essential things like good sanitary facilities in the camp. Gandhi wanted to teach them a lesson. On his own he quietly started cleaning the bathroom and latrine. No one volunteered to join him.

"Why do you undertake an untouchable's job?" they asked.

"Because the caste people have made this an untouchable place," replied Gandhi.

From Calcutta Gandhi travelled across India by train. As he moved from place to place, he was shocked to see the life of the common people—the famished, ignorant and neglected masses. His heart was filled with sadness and anger.

Gandhi settled down in Bombay and started practice as a lawyer. He did well, much better than he had expected.

In December 1902, however, a cable reached him from South Africa requesting him to return as promised. Joseph Chamberlain, the Secretary of State for the Colonies was arriving from London on a visit to Natal and the Transvaal and the Natal Indian Congress wanted Gandhi to present their case to him.

9

Gandhi kept his promise. He reached Natal in time to lead the Indian deputation, but Joseph Chamberlain gave the deputation a cold reception. The Indians felt disheartened. From Natal, Chamberlain proceeded to the Transvaal. The Indians there also wanted Gandhi to present their grievances to him.

Before the Boer war, Indians had been free to enter the Transvaal at any time, but now they had to obtain a permit from the newly-created Asiatic Department. The new rule was designed to separate Indians from the whites. To get a permit was no easy matter.

The officers of the Asiatic Department did their best to prevent Gandhi from entering the Transvaal but he had his way in the end. He got a permit and went to Pretoria. But he was not allowed to lead a deputation and present the memorandum he had drafted.

Gandhi now decided to stay in the Transvaal and fight the colour bar which was taking an ugly shape there. He realized that now he would not be able to leave the country as he had hoped to do. He, therefore, settled down and prepared to do his utmost for the cause of the coloured people, particularly his countrymen.

He was enrolled in the Supreme Court at Johannesburg. He rented a place and established his office. He made good earnings from his practice, but his heart was in the service of the people.

Meanwhile, he continued his experiments with vegetarianism. He gave up all luxuries and pleasures. His idea was to tune his physical body to his spiritual self.

It was at this time that a friend, Madanjit, came to Gandhi with a proposal to start a journal called *Indian Opinion.* Gandhi liked the idea and in 1904 the journal was launched. Mansukhlal Naazar was the editor. Gandhi helped the journal generously, contributing money from his own earnings. He also organized the work and wrote the editorial column. The journal, published every week in Gujarati and English, reflected his ideals and gave the Indian readers a liberal education. With absolute frankness Gandhi pointed out to them their failings and prejudices. *Indian Opinion* also gave the Europeans a correct picture of the difficulties faced by the Indians in South Africa.

With his office colleagues in Johannesburg, 1906

After the rains in 1904 there was a sudden outbreak of plague in one of the gold-mining areas near Johannesburg. It soon spread to the Indian quarters. Gandhi rushed to the spot and organized preventive measures. With the help of friends, he set up improvized hospitals and looked after the sick.

Another thing that happened that year was that Gandhi met H.S.L. Polak, then a sub-editor of *The Critic*. The two soon became good friends as their outlook on life was similar.

Polak presented to Gandhi a copy of *Unto This Last*, a book written by John Ruskin. This book on economics presented many new ideas and it influenced Gandhi a great deal. He then hit upon the idea of starting a farm and founding a community with a true sense of brotherhood. His friends supported the project enthusiastically.

About a hundred acres of land were acquired at a place called Phoenix near Durban and a farm was set up. In the beginning six families settled there. *Indian Opinion* was moved to Phoenix, complete with press and office. Members of any race could freely go and live there, cultivating the soil or working at the press.

Gandhi, however, could stay in the Phoenix Settlement only for brief periods. His headquarters were at Johannesburg where he continued his practice as a lawyer. He knew that it would not be possible to return to India in the near future, so he decided to send for Kasturbai and the children. They soon joined him.

Whenever he found time he undertook the task of educating his three sons. He also pursued the experiments with his diet.

"I intend to be the ruler of my body," he would say. "The

spirit can only rule me if I am free of earthly wants."

He gave up coffee and tea. Next, he gave up milk. Sometimes he would forgo all food and take only water. Kasturbai watched all this silently. She knew it was useless to argue with her husband on such matters.

In 1906 the Zulu Rebellion broke out in Natal. It was a no-tax campaign. The Zulus were only asserting their rights but the whites got panicky and declared war against the Zulus.

Gandhi's sympathies were with the Zulus, but they were fighting against the British and Gandhi believed that the British Empire existed for the welfare of the world. He considered it his duty to help the British. He offered to

form an Indian Ambulance Corps. The authorities accepted the offer.

The Indian Ambulance Corps consisted of a squad of 24 men, and was in active service for six weeks, nursing and looking after the wounded.

Gandhi realized that the whites were determined to enforce the tax on the unwilling Zulus. They wanted to put down all resistance and deny the coloured people their rights in their own land.

The Zulu Rebellion was finally over and Gandhi returned to Johannesburg. His presence was needed there to look after the interests of the Indians, for they were facing all kinds of oppression from the white settlers.

Service medals awarded to Gandhi for his services during Boer War and the Zulu Rebellion in South Africa, 1906

10

In August 1906 an ordinance—Black Act—was issued by the Transvaal Government requiring all Indians—men, women and children—to register themselves and obtain a personal certificate bearing name and thumb impression. This card was to be carried by all individuals at all times and had to be shown on demand. Anyone failing to produce the certificate was liable to be fined, imprisoned, or deported. The police even had orders to enter private houses and check certificates.

"This is too much to bear," Gandhi told his co-workers. "If we meekly submit, it will spell absolute ruin for us in South Africa. We must take action immediately if we are to live here."

The Indians decided not to submit to this humiliating and insulting measure. They must fight it. But, how?

Gandhi saw here the need for passive resistance or satyagraha. He explained to the people his concept of satyagraha. First, he said, they must be prepared to observe absolute non-violence. The authorities would take all measures to put down the agitation. They might use violence, arrest people and send them to jail, but all this must be faced without resistance.

"Merely disobeying the government's laws will not be enough." Gandhi said. "You must have no hatred in your hearts. And you must cast away all fear."

The government ignored all the protests against the ordinance and it came into force. The Indians decided to disobey the provisions of the Black Act. Hundreds of Indians were arrested, tried and imprisoned. They all pleaded guilty and went to jail without putting up any defence.

Gandhi too was imprisoned. Then one day he was taken out of prison and sent to Pretoria to see General Smuts.

"This movement you have started," Smuts said, "must stop at once. It is not in me to dislike Indians, but they must obey the law."

"I would rather die than submit to this law," Gandhi replied. "It is meant to humiliate the Indians."

After some argument, however, Smuts and Gandhi reached a compromise. While Gandhi promised to end the satyagraha if the Black Act was repealed and the prisoners released, Smuts agreed to do this provided the Indians would register of their own accord. On this agreement, they parted.

Back in Johannesburg, Gandhi called a meeting of the Indians.

"We must now register voluntarily to show that we do not intend to bring a single Indian to the Transvaal by fraud," he said. "If we show our goodwill by prompt registration, General Smuts will see that the Black Act is repealed."

Most of the Indians agreed with Gandhi, but a Pathan named Mir Alam shouted at him: "It was you who told us that fingerprints were required only from criminals. It was you who said we must disobey the Black Act. How does all that fit into your attitude today?"

The next morning Gandhi, with his fellow satyagrahis, set out for the registration office. But on the way Mir Alam attacked him. Gandhi fell down unconscious. Mir Alam and his associates went on beating him until he was rescued by some friends. When Gandhi recovered consciousness, he found himself in the house of an Englishman.

Struggling to sit up, Gandhi said in a weak voice, "Do not blame Mir Alam, for he did not understand."

Then he insisted that a clerk from the registration office should come to take his thumb impression and make out his certificate. Many Indians followed Gandhi by registering voluntarily.

But General Smuts did not repeal the Black Act.

The Indians, disappointed at the government's attitude, demanded a return of their applications for voluntary registration.

Still the Transvaal Government did not budge.

Gandhi, who had by then recovered from his injuries, gave an ultimatum: "If the Black Act is not repealed before a fixed date, the certificates collected by the Indians will be burnt."

When he found that the government ignored this threat, Gandhi started another satyagraha movement. A big bonfire was lit and more than two thousand certificates were burnt. Many Indians openly crossed the border into the Transvaal, where their presence was illegal. Gandhi and many of his compatriots were imprisoned several times in the course of the agitation. When Gandhi came out of jail for the third time, the Indians held a meeting and decided to send a deputation to England to acquaint the British Government

with the real situation in South Africa. Gandhi and Seth
Haji Habib were asked to go to London and present the
grievances of the Indians. Accordingly they went, but the
mission was a failure. They returned with grim determination to fight till the end.

Gandhi then made a big decision. He gave up his practice
as a lawyer. He felt he could not go on earning his living by law
when he was defying it.

*As a satyagrahi in
South Africa, 1913*

11

Hermann Kallenbach, a white farmer, was so impressed with the peaceful way of life at Phoenix that he offered Gandhi his own big farm near Johannesburg to start another colony. He suggested that all those who had lost their jobs and homes by their participation in the satyagraha could be settled there.

The new colony was established in 1910 and named 'Tolstoy Farm', after the great Russian writer whom Gandhi much admired. Here people who were different in nationality, religion and colour lived together like one family. They worked hard and shared the fruits of their labour.

Gandhi spent much of his time at Tolstoy Farm. He was engaged in teaching the children, and in other constructive activities.

Gandhi's efforts to persuade General Smuts to change the attitude of the government towards the Indians had failed. Meanwhile, the struggle continued against the Black Act and the poll-tax. And now hundreds of Indian women, including Kasturbai, joined the movement.

There had been a recent court decision in South Africa holding that Indian marriages were not recognized by law. The women could not brook this attack on family ties. They openly broke the law and were imprisoned in large numbers. In the coal mines at Newcastle, in Natal, Indian workers went on strike protesting against the repression.

The arrests, the deportation of passive-resisters and the untold sufferings of Indian families, angered the people of India. A large amount of money was collected for the relief of the victims.

Many satyagrahis were beaten and flogged and some were even killed. Gandhi, who felt intensely the humiliation his people suffered, took a triple vow of self-suffering. He decided to dress like a poor labourer, to walk bare-foot, and to have only one meal a day, till the poll-tax and other injustices were abolished.

Gandhi found the government relentless. There was no solution in sight. He had to take further measures.

In October 1913 Gandhi organized a march of over 6,000 Indian workers from the Natal mining area into the Transvaal, although crossing into the Transvaal without a permit was not allowed by law.

Gandhi said, "We are going to march peacefully together across the border into the Transvaal. The government will arrest us and put us in prison. We are to remain peaceful. This is the non-violent way of protesting against the poll-tax, against the government's decision not to recognize our marriages, and against all the laws that are made against us. We are fighting for just causes, we will not harm anyone."

He then cried to the people, "Are you ready to face arrest and harsh treatment, remaining always non-violent?"

Roars of assent assured him of everyone's support. They

were ready to follow Gandhi anywhere. And so the march into the Transvaal began.

Late in the evening Gandhi was roused from sleep by several uniformed men.

"I know," he said, "you have come to arrest me. I am ready."

Gandhi and many other Indians were imprisoned. The mines were surrounded with barbed wire and converted into temporary jails. The satyagrahis were beaten and flogged to force them to go back to work, but without success. The authorities could not make them return to work. Gandhi had aroused in them the spirit of quiet, dignified resistance.

Soon the movement of passive resistance or satyagraha spread all through Natal and the Transvaal. The government did not know what to do because none yielded to their cruel treatment. The prisons were overflowing. At last General Smuts was obliged to act. He appointed a Commission to study the situation.

In December 1913 Gandhi was released, but he would not give up the struggle.

Gandhi threatened Smuts that he would start another march if his demands were not met. That march, however, never took place.

The European employees of the railways in the Union went on strike and this made the government's position extremely difficult. Gandhi decided to drop the idea of the march at such a critical time as he did not wish to embarrass the government further.

Gandhi ordered every Indian to go back to work, at least for the time being. His decision created a good impression on the government and even General Smuts recognized this courtesy.

The Inquiry Commission reported in favour of all the essential reforms demanded by the Indian leaders. The Indians' Relief Bill was at last passed and signed by the Governor. It abolished the poll-tax on indentured workers, declared absolutely legal all Indian marriages, and removed penalties for crossing from one State to another.

Gandhi had won. And so had the satyagraha movement.

Gandhi had been active in South Africa for 21 years and had contributed much to the welfare of the Indians in South Africa.

With Kasturbai in South Africa, 1914

12

Gandhi now felt that his mission in South Africa was over and he wanted to return to India.

At that time Gopal Krishna Gokhale was in England. He wanted Gandhi to meet him in London before returning to India. Gandhi promised to do so.

Gandhi announced his decision to Kasturbai.

"You are going to London with me," he said. "From England we will go back to India."

Gandhi, with Kasturbai and Kallenbach, sailed for England on July 18, 1914. On August 4, two days before he reached London, the First World War was declared.

On arrival in London, Gandhi heard that Gokhale had gone to Paris for reasons of health. Communications were cut off between London and Paris because of the war. Gandhi was disappointed. He did not want to return to India without seeing Gokhale, so he stayed on in London.

The war was on. What could Gandhi do in England? At the suggestion of some Indian friends, a meeting was called of the Indians in England. Gandhi expressed the view that Indians residing in England ought to do their bit in the war.

English students had volunteered to serve in the army and Indians should do no less.

There were objections to his views and many Indians were of the opinion that the war provided an opportunity to get freedom for India and that Indians should assert themselves and claim their rights.

Gandhi felt that England's difficulty should not be turned into India's opportunity. He insisted on rendering all possible help to England. He organized an ambulance corps which, in spite of all difficulties, helped the British in their time of need.

After some time Gokhale returned to England. Gandhi and Kallenbach went to see him often and they talked together about the war and other matters.

Then Gandhi had an attack of pleurisy and Gokhale and his friends were worried. Dr. Jivraj Mehta treated Gandhi but there was little relief. Gandhi was still ill when Gokhale returned to India.

As the pleurisy still persisted, Gandhi was advised to go back to India as soon as possible. He accepted the advice and returned to India.

13

Gandhi was back in India after twelve long years.

A great reception awaited him in Bombay. Gandhi was overwhelmed by the great love shown to him by the people. Gokhale was in Poona (now Pune) and he was in poor health, so Gandhi went to see him. He was received with great affection. Gandhi told Gokhale that his plan was to build an ashram where he could settle down with his Phoenix family. They had already reached India and were at Santiniketan. Gokhale approved of the idea and promised whatever help he could give.

Gandhi went to Rajkot and Porbandar to meet his relatives and then went on to Santiniketan. The teachers and students gave him a warm welcome. There Gandhi met Tagore for the first time, and also C.F. Andrews who was visiting Santiniketan.

During his short stay at Santiniketan Gandhi heard the sad news that Gokhale had passed away. He immediately left for Poona. C.F. Andrews accompanied him as far as Burdwan.

"Do you think," Andrews asked Gandhi, "that a time will

come for satyagraha in India? If so, how soon will it be?"

"It is difficult to say," replied Gandhi. "For one year I am to do nothing. Gokhale made me promise that I would travel in India for one year to gain experience, and that I would express no opinion until I had finished this period of probation. So I do not think there will be any occasion for satyagraha for five years."

After attending the shraddha ceremony of Gokhale, Gandhi met the leaders of the Servants of India Society. Out of respect for Gokhale Gandhi would have joined the Society, but there was opposition from a certain section of the members.

Gandhi visited Rangoon (now Yangoon) for a short period and on his return he went to Hardwar during the time of the Kumbha Fair. About seventeen hundred thousand people attended the Fair. Volunteer corps from different organizations had gone to Hardwar to be of service to the big crowds that were flowing in. Gandhi was invited to go there with the Phoenix party to help the volunteers. The

With Kasturbai and children at a reception in Ahmedabad, 1915

With Rabindranath Tagore and C.F. Andrews, 1925

Phoenix group went there and Gandhi joined them. Gandhi was pained at the many happenings and shortcomings at the great religious fair. There was corruption, cheating, and many other anti-social activities. Scant care was taken about sanitary arrangements.

All this made Gandhi feel very sad. He thought a great deal about the problem of how to improve the Indian character.

In May 1915 an ashram was established in a village near Ahmedabad. Ahmedabad was an ancient centre of handloom weaving and Gandhi thought the place was suited for the revival of the cottage industry of hand-spinning. Gandhi named the new institution 'Satyagraha Ashram'.

"Our creed is devotion to truth, and our business is the search for and insistence on truth," he said.

A simple uniform style of clothing was worn by all who

were there. They took their food together in a common kitchen and strived to live as one family.

Gandhi told the members: "If you want to serve the people, it is essential to observe the vows of truth, ahimsa,

With Kasturbai, 1915

celibacy, non-stealing, non-possession, and control of the palate."

One day Gandhi said to the members of the ashram, "I have received an application from an untouchable family who want to join us here. I am replying that they are welcome."

This created quite a flutter. To live with untouchables! Even Kasturbai had her misgivings. Gandhi's mind was made up, however, and there could be no objection from the members of the ashram. But the patrons of the ashram did not like the idea and they stopped their monetary help.

The ashram was faced with a financial crisis, but help came unexpectedly. A rich man came to the ashram and gave Gandhi ₹13,000. Gandhi was surprised at his magnanimous gesture.

14

In February 1916, Gandhi was invited to speak at the laying of the foundation stone of the Banaras Hindu University. The Viceroy and many of the most important people of India were there. Gandhi, clad in a Kathiawadi long coat and a turban, rose to speak. The police arrangements and also the pomp and luxury around him, hurt him deeply. Turning to the audience he said, "I want to think audibly and speak without reserve."

His first words froze the audience.

"It is a matter of deep humiliation and shame for us," he said, "that I am compelled this evening, under the shadow of this great college in this sacred city, to address my countrymen in a language that is foreign to me."

It was a bomb-shell. Nobody had ever dared to speak against the English language. The British officers, their friends, and the important Indians who had gathered there were breathing heavily in anger.

But Gandhi went on, "His Highness, the Maharaja who presided yesterday over our deliberations, spoke about the poverty of India. But what did we witness? A most gorgeous show, an exhibition of jewellery... There is no salvation for India unless you strip yourselves of this jewellery and hold it in trust for your countrymen in India."

Gandhi gave a long speech, covering many topics. His speech was full of outspoken criticism.

Mrs. Annie Besant, who was one of the organizers of the function, was horrified and urged Gandhi to sit down. But Gandhi went on. Some people went red with rage, but others listened to Gandhi with the greatest interest.

"Here at last is a man telling the truth," they thought. "He is the man to raise India from the mire."

They applauded him and shouted joyfully.

Gandhi turned to them and said, "No amount of speeches will ever make us fit for self-government. It is only our conduct that will fit us for it."

Gandhi told them that they should all be the kind of people able to take up the work of self-government.

Finally, Gandhi, the man who had supported the British thrice in their war efforts said, "If I found it necessary for the salvation of India that the English should retire, that they should be driven out, I would not hesitate to declare that they would have to go, and I hope I would be prepared to die in defence of that belief..."

The people were amazed at Gandhi's frankness. It was Gandhi's first great political speech in India.

Years later Jawaharlal described what the coming of Gandhi meant to the Indian people.

He said, "We seemed to be helpless in the grip of some all-powerful monster; our limbs were paralysed, our minds deadened... What could we do? How could we pull India out of this quagmire of poverty and defeatism which sucked her in?"

"And then Gandhi came. He was like a powerful current of fresh air that made us stretch ourselves and take deep breaths, like a beam of light that pierced the darkness and removed the scales from our eyes, like a whirlwind that upset many things, but most of all the working of people's minds."

Several conferences demanding Home Rule were held in India during the latter half of 1916. They marked a new wave of political life under the leadership of Bal Gangadhar Tilak, Annie Besant and Jinnah.

The annual meeting of the Congress was held in December that year in Lucknow. The Congress was divided. There were the moderates and there were the extremists, but at Lucknow the Congress met without tension between the two wings.

The President, Ambika Charan Mazumdar, spoke in terms of Swaraj, which previous leaders had demanded. A resolution was passed appealing to His Majesty's Government and demanding that a definite step should be taken towards Indian self-government by granting the reforms contained in the scheme prepared by the All-India Congress Committee and adopted by the All-India Muslim League.

In Lucknow the Congress and the Muslim League came to an agreement. This was afterwards known as the Lucknow Pact. For the sake of the unity of India the Congress conceded many points demanded by the Muslims.

For two years Gandhi had travelled extensively and had talked at different places. He now wanted to start some work connected with labour. His interest first centred in the problem of indentured labour, the system under which poor, ignorant labourers were enticed away from India to work in the British colonies. He had fought this system in South Africa and he wanted to see it abolished.

The Viceroy, Lord Hardinge, announced that His Majesty's Government had agreed to abolish the system in due course.

Gandhi, however, wanted a definite date before which the system would go.

So now Gandhi started a massive agitation on this issue. He went to Bombay and consulted all the Indian leaders there. They fixed May 31, 1917 as the last date for the abolition of indentured labour. He then went round the country to get support for this view.

Meetings were held in all important places. Everywhere there was a great response. Even Gandhi said that he had not expected so much public support.

As a result of the agitation, the government announced that the system of indentured labour would be stopped before July 31, 1917.

With Chittaranjan Das (seen behind him, second from left) in Darjeeling, 1925

15

Now Gandhi heard about an obnoxious system of agricultural labour prevailing in Bihar.

In the Champaran district of Bihar, the cultivators were forced by Europeans to grow indigo, a blue dye, and this imposed on them untold sufferings. They could not grow the food they needed, nor did they receive adequate payment for the indigo.

Gandhi was unaware of this until an agriculturist from Bihar, Rajkumar Shukla, met him and told him of the woes of the people of Champaran. He requested Gandhi to go to the place and see for himself the state of affairs there. Gandhi was then attending the Congress meeting at Lucknow and he did not have time to go there. Rajkumar Shukla followed him about, begging him to come and help the suffering villagers in Champaran. Gandhi at last promised to visit the place after he had visited Calcutta.

When Gandhi was in Calcutta, Rajkumar was there too, to take him to Bihar.

Gandhi went to Champaran with Rajkumar early in 1917. On his arrival, the District Magistrate served him with a notice saying that he was not to remain in the district of Champaran, but must leave the place by the first available train.

Gandhi did not obey this order. He was summoned to appear before the court.

The magistrate said, "If you leave the district now and promise not to return, the case against you will be withdrawn."

"This cannot be," replied Gandhi. "I came here to render humanitarian and national service. I shall make Champaran my home and work for the suffering people."

A large crowd of peasants was outside the court shouting slogans. The magistrate and the police looked nervous.

Then Gandhi said, "I shall help you to calm these people if I can speak to them."

Gandhi appeared before the crowd and said, "You must show your faith in me and in my work by remaining quiet. The magistrate had the right to arrest me, because I disobeyed his order. If I am sent to jail, you must accept that as just. We must work peacefully. Any violent act will harm our cause."

The crowd dispersed peacefully. The police stared at Gandhi in admiration as he went inside the court.

The government withdrew the case against Gandhi and allowed him to remain in the district. Gandhi stayed there to study the grievances of the peasants.

He visited many villages. He cross-examined about 8,000 cultivators and recorded their statements. In this way he arrived at an exact understanding of their grievances and the causes underlying them.

He came to the conclusion that the ignorance of the cultivators was one of the main reasons why it was possible for the European planters to repress them. Gandhi, therefore, set up voluntary organizations to improve the economic and educational conditions of the people. They opened schools and also taught the people how to improve sanitation.

The government realized Gandhi's strength and his devotion to causes. They themselves then set up a committee to enquire into the grievances of the cultivators. They invited Gandhi to serve on that committee, and he agreed. The result was that within a few months the Champaran Agrarian Bill was passed. It gave immense relief to the cultivators and land-tenants.

Gandhi could not stay longer in Bihar. There were calls from other places. Labour unrest was brewing in Ahmedabad and Gandhi was requested to help settle the dispute.

16

Gandhi hurried back to Ahmedabad.

Before taking up the labour dispute Gandhi wanted to move his ashram. The Satyagraha Ashram was in a village near Ahmedabad, but the surroundings were not clean leading to an outbreak of plague that had spread there from Ahmedabad.

A rich merchant of Ahmedabad who was closely associated with the ashram, volunteered to procure a suitable piece of land. Gandhi moved about with him looking for land and at last they chose a place on the banks of the Sabarmati River, near the Sabarmati Central Jail. The land was purchased and there the famous Sabarmati Ashram was started.

In Ahmedabad there were many textile mills. Prices had gone up and the mill workers were demanding higher wages. The mill owners would not agree. Gandhi sympathized with the workers and took up their cause. He launched a struggle and resorted to peaceful resistance. The workers proudly followed Gandhi and pledged their full support to him. They paraded the streets with large banners and said they would not go back to work until a settlement had been reached.

Days passed. The mill owners were adamant. The strikers were getting impatient for they were faced with starvation. Their discipline became weak. Gandhi feared that some workers would break their pledge and go back to work. That would be a great moral defeat.

One morning he called the workers and said, "Unless the strikers rally and continue the strike till a settlement is reached, I will not touch any food."

The workers were shocked.

"Not you, but we shall fast," they said. "Please forgive us for our lapse; we shall remain faithful to our pledge."

Gandhi did not want anybody else to fast. His fast was not against the mill owners, but against the lack of co-ordination and unity among the workers. The fast lasted only for three days. It influenced the mill owners so much that they came to an agreement with the workers.

Hardly was the mill workers' strike over, when Gandhi had to plunge into the Kheda satyagraha struggle.

The Kheda district of Gujarat was on the verge of famine owing to failure of the crops. The yield had been so low that the cultivators, especially the poorer section, were unable to pay the revenue. But the government insisted that the yield had not been so bad and that the cultivators should pay the tax.

Gandhi saw the justice of the cause of the cultivators and advised them to offer satyagraha by not paying their taxes.

Many leaders, like Vallabhbhai Patel, Shankarlal Banker, Mahadev Desai and others, took an active part in this struggle. The campaign came to an unexpected end. There had been signs that it might fizzle out, but after four months' struggle there came an honourable settlement. The government said that if well-to-do cultivators paid up, the poorer section would be granted exemption. This was agreed to and the campaign ended.

The Kheda satyagraha marked the beginning of an awakening among the peasants of Gujarat, the beginning of their true political education. In addition it gave to the educated public workers the chance to establish contact with the actual life of the peasants.

17

During this time the war had entered a critical phase. Britain and France were in a difficult position. In the spring of 1917 Germany had inflicted crushing defeats on both the British and French troops in France. Russia's war efforts had broken down and the revolution was threatening its government. Though America had entered the war, no American troops had yet reached the battle-front.

The Viceroy of India, Lord Chelmsford, invited various Indian leaders to attend a War Conference. Gandhi was also invited. He accepted the invitation and went to Delhi. Gandhi was not happy that leaders like Tilak or the Ali brothers had not been invited to the conference, so he felt unwilling to attend. After meeting the Viceroy, however, he attended the conference.

The Viceroy was very keen that Gandhi should support the resolution on recruiting.

Gandhi spoke only one sentence: "With a full sense of my responsibility I beg to support the resolution."

Gandhi had supported the government's resolution on recruiting! Many of his friends were taken aback.

Some said, "You are a votary of ahimsa: how can you ask us to take up arms?"

Others said, "What good has the government done to India to deserve our cooperation?"

Even some of his best friends could not understand how he could reconcile the war effort with his campaign for ahimsa.

But Gandhi stuck to the belief he held at that time that 'absolutely unconditional and whole-hearted cooperation with the government on the part of educated India will bring us within sight of our goal of Swaraj as nothing else will'.

Gandhi had made his decision and he now set out to implement it.

The response to recruitment was not in any way encouraging, but Gandhi was determined to carry out his mission. He held meetings. He issued leaflets asking people to enlist in the forces. His steady work began to bear fruit. Many men were recruited and he hoped to get a bigger response as soon as the first batch had been sent.

Gandhi nearly ruined his health during the recruitment campaign. He worked very hard. He could not take his food at regular times, nor could he take enough nourishment to keep up his energy.

He had an attack of dysentery. He refused to take medicines and his condition became worse. Friends tried their best to advise him but he was beyond all advice. He passed restless days and nights and he himself felt at times that he was near death's door.

It took him a long time to regain his health, but before that the news came that the war was over. Germany had been completely defeated.

There was now no need for any further recruitment.

Friends and doctors advised him to go away for a change and recover his health. He went to Matheran in Maharashtra, but the place did not suit him.

He went to Poona, where a doctor was consulted. He advised Gandhi to take milk to rebuild his body, and also prescribed a few injections. Gandhi agreed to take the injections but he did not agree to drink milk, for he had given up milk years ago.

But Kasturbai said, "Your objection is to cow and buffalo milk. You cannot object to taking goat's milk."

"If you consume goat's milk, it will be good enough," said the doctor.

Gandhi agreed to drink goat's milk.

Gandhi returned to Ahmedabad. He was recouping his health there when he read in the papers the Rowlatt Committee's report which had just been published.

This report recommended the introduction of amendments to the criminal law. These recommendations startled Gandhi. He described them as "unjust, subversive of the principles of liberty and justice, and destructive of the elementary rights of individuals".

Friends approached Gandhi for guidance.

"Something must be done," he said to them. "If the proposed measures are passed into law, we ought to do a satyagraha."

Gandhi was sorry he was in poor health, else he would have put up resistance against the amendments alone. From his sickbed he wrote articles for the Indian papers explaining that the proposed bill was an act of tyranny. No self-respecting people could submit to it.

Gandhi thought that the only possible step against the

government's proposal would be to start the satyagraha movement in right earnest. A meeting of some of the leaders was called at the ashram and a satyagraha pledge was drafted. It was signed by all those present there.

Gandhi did not believe that the existing institutions could handle such a noble weapon, so a separate institution named Satyagraha Sabha was formed. Its headquarters were in Bombay.

There were agitations everywhere against the Rowlatt Committee's report. But the government was determined to give effect to its recommendations, and in 1919 the Rowlatt Bill was introduced. When the bill was debated in India's Legislative Chamber, Gandhi attended as a visitor.

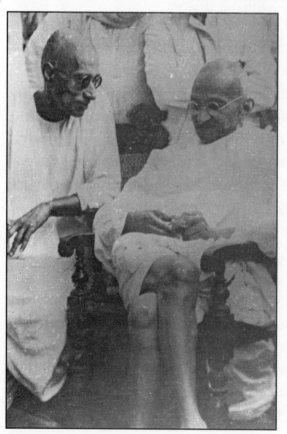

In spite of all the opposition from national-minded people, the bill was passed and it became law.

Gandhi was still in a weak physical condition when he received an invitation to go to Madras (now Chennai).

He took the risk and went to Madras with Mahadev Desai.

It was there that he first met Chakravarthi

With C. Rajagopalachari on his tour to Madras, 1937

Rajagopalachari, who impressed him very much.

A small conference of leaders was held and Gandhi explained to them the implications of the Rowlatt Bill. While these discussions were being held, news was received that the Rowlatt Bill had been published as an act.

It was also in Madras that Gandhi first conceived the idea of an All India hartal as the beginning of the satyagraha movement. The leaders at once took up the suggestion and gave much publicity to the forthcoming hartal. The date was first fixed for March 30, 1919, but was subsequently changed to April 6. While the people had received only a short notice for the hartal, it turned out to be most successful.

That was the first great awakening of India in her struggle towards Independence.

Gandhi left Madras and went to Bombay to join in the hartal there on April 6.

Meanwhile in Delhi, Lahore and Amritsar, the hartal had been observed on March 30. In Delhi the police did not allow free movement to the demonstrators and there was firing, causing a number of casualties. Gandhi was requested to go to Delhi and he replied that he would do so after the hartal in Bombay on April 6.

In Bombay the hartal was a great success. Not a wheel turned in any factory. Not a shop was kept open.

All over India the hartal was observed. Gandhi had asked the people again and again to be peaceful and not to be provoked to violence by the Government's actions. In spite of this, violence broke out in many places. There were disturbances in Ahmedabad and also in the Punjab and he decided to go to these places to propagate non-violence.

On the way to the Punjab he was arrested at a wayside

station called Palwal and sent back to Bombay. The news of his arrest inflamed the entire population of Bombay.

There was an enormous crowd awaiting his arrival there. When he reached Bombay, he was set free. The crowd was getting impatient.

"Only you can control the crowd," said a friend to Gandhi. "Come, I shall take you to the spot."

The crowd greeted Gandhi with frenzied joy. A huge procession started, but the police barred its progress. A troop of mounted police was ordered to charge. Piercing screams and cries from women and children filled the air as the horsemen plunged forward with lowered lances. People ran to escape the fury of the police.

Gandhi was shocked. He went and met the Commissioner. He found him boiling with rage.

"We, the police, know better than you of the effect of your preaching on the people. If we had not taken drastic measures, the situation would have passed out of our hands. I have no doubt about your intentions, but the people do not understand them. They only follow their natural instincts."

"The people by nature are not violent but peaceful," said Gandhi.

"You wanted to go to the Punjab," said the Commissioner. "Do you know what is happening in Ahmedabad, Punjab and Delhi? You are responsible for all these disturbances."

Gandhi was pained to hear of the disturbances and said that he would certainly claim responsibility if he was convinced that it was his doing.

Gandhi went to Ahmedabad. On the way he learnt in detail about the happenings there. Ahmedabad was under martial law.

A police officer was waiting for him at the railway station to escort him to the Commissioner. This Commissioner too was in a rage. Gandhi expressed his regret for the disturbances and promised complete cooperation in restoring peace.

Gandhi then asked for permission to hold a public meeting on the grounds of Sabarmati Ashram. The proposal appealed to the officer.

At the meeting Gandhi announced with great sorrow the suspension of civil disobedience. He said he would fast for three days as a penance and he appealed to all the people to fast for one day. He asked those who were guilty of violence to confess their guilt. He expressed his regret at having started civil disobedience too early without giving sufficient training to the people.

"I have made a Himalayan miscalculation," he said.

Many people jeered at Gandhi for saying that. Many of his friends and followers were furious at his stopping the satyagraha.

Gandhi then started teaching people the true meaning of satyagraha and how it should be conducted. Through his articles and speeches he wanted to drive home to the people the essence of his new creed.

18

In the Punjab the situation was very critical. It was true that there were disturbances on the part of the people, but the measures adopted by the government to check the disturbances were too severe.

The leaders were trying to keep the people peaceful, but the stern measures of repression taken by the authorities had few parallels in history.

In Amritsar the people were not allowed to move about freely. A proclamation was issued forbidding all gatherings and meetings. Only a few had the chance to know about the proclamation, however, because it was not announced widely besides, it was made only in English.

It was announced that a meeting was to be held in a garden called Jallianwala Bagh, to make a protest against the Government's actions. General Dyer took no measures to prevent the meeting. However, he reached the place soon after the meeting began with armoured cars and troops. Without giving any warning he ordered, "Fire till the ammunition is exhausted."

The garden was surrounded by walls and buildings and

The Jallianwala Bagh massacre (from a painting in the library of the Golden Temple, Amritsar)

had only one exit. At the first shot the exit was jammed and there was no hope of escape for the crowd. There were more than ten thousand people there. The soldiers fired over sixteen hundred rounds at the unarmed mass of people.

Once a public garden, the Jallianwala Bagh was now a scene of merciless massacre where hundreds of men, women, and children were butchered. However, the official figures given were: 379 killed and 200 wounded. Leaving the wounded and the dying on the ground, the troops marched away. The words, 'Jallianwala Bagh' had now become synonymous with massacre.

Bad as this was, there were other even more shameful deeds executed all over the Punjab. Indians were ordered to crawl on their hands and knees. In addition General Dyer ordered that in certain areas all Indians were to alight from vehicles and salute whenever they passed a British officer. Furthermore, at certain places men were stripped naked and flogged. Students and children were ordered to walk miles for a roll call, to attend parades, and to salute the British flag. Then there was the stripping and flogging of people going to marriage parties, the censorship of communications, and cutting of water and electricity supplies to Indian families. The administration of General Dyer's martial law created a reign of terror in the Punjab.

C.F. Andrews, who had already reached the Punjab, wrote to Gandhi and begged him to come at once. Gandhi was equally keen to go, but his repeated requests for permission to visit the place were turned down by the government. Finally, in October that year, the Viceroy granted him permission to visit the Punjab and Gandhi immediately proceeded.

On his arrival at the Lahore railway station, Gandhi found that almost the entire population of the city was there waiting for him.

The Congress had appointed a committee to enquire into the atrocities committed in the Punjab. Gandhi was requested to join the committee now that he was there. He started a slow but most methodical investigation of the incidents in the Punjab.

Gandhi thus had the opportunity to know the Punjab and its people. The people flocked to him. They loved him and respected him.

Jawaharlal Nehru, who was also there in the Punjab, realized that Gandhi was the leader of the masses. People were drawn to him because of his thoughts and deeds. Nehru saw the scientific accuracy with which Gandhi was conducting the enquiry.

Gandhi's report of the atrocities showed that efforts were

being made by the government to shield certain persons.

Gandhi was never interested in taking revenge on anybody but he was shocked at the way the government sat silent when its own report was published.

Gandhi was very much moved by the sufferings of the people in the Punjab. He knew the extent of the atrocities committed on defenceless people.

Gandhi now advised the people to non-cooperate with the government in every possible way. He advised them not to accept any of the honours offered by Britain, and requested those who had already received honours to return them. He wanted people to start a movement to boycott the law courts. He advised people not to buy any foreign goods. He wanted every effort to be made to persuade Indians not to serve the government in any capacity. He called out students from educational institutions.

Gandhi's influence on the Indian people was steadily growing. The old leaders, many of them with liberal policies, were vanishing from Indian politics. By the close of 1920 Gandhi was the undisputed leader, and head of the Indian National Congress.

The Congress was fighting for immediate Home Rule. Its method of fighting was non-violent non-cooperation with the government, and defying carefully selected laws at suitable times.

Gandhi was much impressed by Jawaharlal Nehru and his socialistic views and particularly more by the account Jawaharlal had given of his contacts with the peasants, the difficulties they were experiencing, and the high taxes they had to pay.

The political situation in India grew worse. The

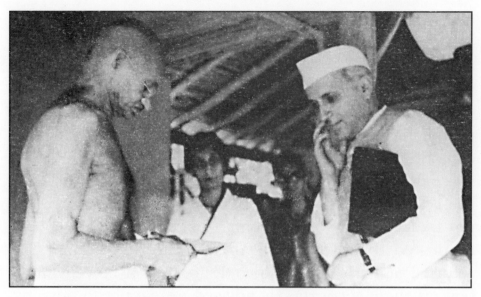

In dicsussion with Jawarharlal Nehru and Rajkumari Amrit Kaur, Seagaon, Maharashtra, 1938

government grew nervous. There was tension everywhere and amidst the suppressed people there was the danger of violence.

In spite of the harsh attitude of the government, Gandhi believed that England would soon right the wrong, before it was too late. Jawaharlal was of the opinion that England would not change her policy unless she was forced to do so. Jawaharlal was right. Soon the government started arresting the leaders and imprisoning them. The British were afraid to loosen their grip on India.

On August 1, 1920, in a letter to the Viceroy, Lord Chelmsford, Gandhi gave the signal for a non-cooperation campaign. Along with it he returned the Kaiser-i-Hind gold medal which had been awarded to him in 1915. In the columns of *Young India* Gandhi wrote in detail in defence of non-violent non-cooperation.

With other leaders he travelled extensively, addressing huge meetings and preaching the essentials of satyagraha.

Everywhere the crowds welcomed him with great love and enthusiasm. Again and again he warned the people against violence. He abhorred mass fury.

"If India has to get her freedom by violence," he said, "let it be by the disciplined violence named war."

At the end of August the Gujarat Political Conference passed a non-cooperation resolution and a special session of the Congress was held in Calcutta

Addressing a meeting wearing the 'Gandhi' cap, 1920

from September 4-9. The draft of the non-cooperation resolution had been prepared by Gandhi.

Gandhi was not sure how much support he would get at the Congress session. When he moved the resolution he said that he knew that it envisaged a policy which was different from the one hitherto followed. He knew that many leaders were dead against it.

"But," he declared, "knowing this I stand before you in fear of God and with a sense of duty to put this before you for your acceptance."

The special Congress session adopted the non-cooperation plan as a means of attaining Swaraj.

During the latter part of 1920 Gandhi advocated a triple

83

boycott. He wanted an absolute boycott of the government and all government institutions, including schools, colleges, and courts. If the people were free of these they could easily have their own schools, colleges and courts, and the power. of the British would collapse at once.

There was much laughter and ridicule from the moderates and the supporters of the British rule. But Gandhi paid no attention to them. Gandhi's activities made the government panicky. They issued a warning that anyone who overstepped the limits of law would be arrested and imprisoned.

Gandhi thought that this warning was a victory for the campaign. He issued instructions which the people were to follow if he were arrested.

On December 26, the Congress session was held in Nagpur. Though there were signs of opposition to Gandhi's policies, his resolution was passed with an overwhelming majority.

The adoption of the new programme at Nagpur was the signal to start the mass movement. Gandhi felt that the complete boycott of all government organizations would give a chance to the Congress to set up a parallel organization, a State within a State, which would lead India to Swaraj.

The Duke of Connaught was sent to India in 1921 to try to pacify the Indians. He came to open the four legislatures in the country which had been introduced as a result of the reforms announced by the King. His coming and going passed off without any material change in the attitude of Indians towards Britain.

Gandhi travelled far and wide, propagating the ideals of non-violence and non-cooperation. Day by day the Indians were getting more and more excited over carrying out Gandhi's programme. Many students left their institutions, many officers resigned from their posts.

With Annie Besant, Srinivasa Shastri and Satyamurti, 1921

The boycott movement gained momentum.

As the people's morale grew, the morale of the government went down. Repression started. Gandhi advised the people to have patience and insisted on non-violence. He saw the weaknesses of the Indians and he urged them to improve. He wanted social reforms and constructive work to be intensively followed.

It was announced that the Prince of Wales was to visit India. Functions were arranged at many places to enable him to meet his loyal subjects.

Gandhi was indignant when he read the announcement in the newspapers.

"Do the British think we are children?" he said. "Do they believe that parades for the Prince will make us forget atrocities in the Punjab or the perpetual delay in granting us Home Rule?"

On Gandhi's advice the Congress declared that all parades, receptions and celebrations in honour of the Prince were to be strictly boycotted.

"We have no grudge against His Royal Highness the Prince of Wales," said Gandhi, "but our ideas are against him as a symbol of oppression. We can show the world that such non-cooperation is just the reverse of the European doctrine of the sword. Let us act in accordance with the holy prophets of old. Non-cooperation without violence is the battle of the brave."

Fearing that there would be disorder when His Royal Highness the Prince of Wales visited various places, the government began severe acts of suppression. Thousands of people were arrested.

The Indian people were so agitated that in city after city there were bonfires, and these bonfires were heaps of foreign cloth, especially British cloth, that was burnt.

On November 17, 1921, the Prince of Wales landed in Bombay. Loyal stooges of Britain went to greet the royal visitor. Those who were observing non-violent non-cooperation did not attack them. However, passion suddenly blazed out. Religious and political hatreds fanned the flames. Riots started, many were killed, much property was destroyed. There was panic in the city.

Gandhi was in Bombay and he rushed to the scene of disorder to stop the rioting. Order was finally restored.

"Every man has the right to his religion and his own political opinion. Satyagraha will never succeed until man understands that," Gandhi announced bitterly.

In other cities the boycott of the Prince's visit was peaceful. As the unfortunate Prince of Wales visited city after city, he was greeted with empty streets. Not a shop was open. The people remained behind closed doors and drawn curtains. This infuriated the British and they called upon the Government of India to mediate.

Motilal Nehru, Jawaharlal, and other leaders were arrested and sentenced to various terms of imprisonment. Yet the determined courage of the people did not abate. They were ready to suffer any penalty for the cause of Home Rule.

Demands had been made to Gandhi that he should start a mass movement for the attainment of Swaraj.

Gandhi decided to act. Preparations were made to start satyagraha in Bardoli. But Gandhi had to stop the campaign suddenly because of what had happened in Bombay and other places.

In Chauri Chaura, near Gorakhpur in U.P., some police-men fired on a crowd which was holding a demonstration against the government. This annoyed the demonstrators to such an extent that they became very violent. They chased the police. The police took refuge in the city hall. The angry mob surrounded the hall and set it on fire. Some policemen were burned to death. Others, trying to escape, were killed by the furious mob outside.

Gandhi was very upset. He thought that it was clear that the people were still not prepared for satyagraha. He stopped the intended satyagraha at Bardoli. His co-workers did not agree with him, but he was adamant. He wanted his followers to start constructive programmes.

Many Indians were sorry for Gandhi's action. They thought that Swaraj was now within their reach and the movement should therefore continue.

The government was playing a waiting game. Instead of thanking Gandhi for stopping the mass movement, they arrested him on charges of sedition and sentenced him to six years' imprisonment. He was removed to Yerawada Central Jail in Poona.

19

In prison Gandhi settled down to a regime of spinning, writing and meditation. The people were disappointed and the government tightened its hold everywhere. Almost all the leaders were put in jail.

Then, in 1924, Gandhi fell ill. He was suffering from appendicitis and was in great pain. The government was alarmed. What would happen if Gandhi died in prison? An urgent operation was arranged which Gandhi agreed to. The operation was successful but his recovery was very slow. The government thought it best to release him, so he was set free. He went to Juhu, near Bombay, for his convalescence.

The non-cooperation movement was at a low ebb. Many Congress leaders were thinking of participating in the Municipal and Provincial Councils which Gandhi had advised them to boycott. Gandhi was not dismayed or discouraged. He decided to leave politics alone for a while and spend his time in bringing about Hindu-Muslim unity and the removal of untouchability.

So for nearly six years Gandhi had little to do with politics.

But he wrote, he lectured and he prayed. He travelled all over India. His influence among the people was steadily growing. Gandhi had not given up the idea of non-violent resistance to British rule. He was merely waiting for the right time.

Jawaharlal Nehru joined Gandhi in many of his travels. Everywhere they were both greeted with great enthusiasm. Jawaharlal was the hope of the younger generation.

In 1928 the Viceroy invited Gandhi to see him. He informed Gandhi of the appointment of an official British Commission, led by Sir John Simon, which would study Indian conditions and recommend political reforms.

"Will there be any Indians on the Commission?" asked Gandhi.

"No," replied the Viceroy.

"That is absurd," said Gandhi. "We must boycott it."

Gandhi advised the people to boycott the Simon Commission and when it arrived in Bombay, a hartal was observed all over India. On its tour through the Indian cities, the Commission was greeted with black-flag demonstrations.

The people shouted, "Simon, go back!"

At many places there were lathi charges and shooting.

The same year the peasants of Bardoli, in Gujarat, were agitated by the enhancement of land taxes. Gandhi made a study of their grievances and advised them to resort to satyagraha and the non-payment of taxes. "They must be non-violent," he said. Vallabhbhai Patel took charge of organizing the resistance.

The government tried all its usual measures to terrorize the people but had to climb down. An enquiry into the grievances was ordered. Vallabhbhai demanded certain

With Vallabhbhai Patel

concessions. Negotiations were going on when Gandhi arrived in Bardoli. Within a short period the government came to terms with the organizers and a settlement was reached.

Now political tension again gained momentum. People everywhere were preparing for a mass struggle.

The Viceroy called a meeting of the Indian leaders. He made the announcement that India would get dominion status similar to that of Canada. Gandhi wanted an immediate plan for the framing of the Constitution.

"Gentlemen," the Viceroy said, "I have no power to promise such things."

Everybody then realized that England was still marking time and was not really willing to part with power.

90

20

A new determination to force the government to act filled the minds of the people.

Jawaharlal Nehru was elected President of the Congress at the behest of Gandhi. A Congress session was held in Lahore on December 31, 1929. A resolution announcing that full independence was India's goal was passed at this session of the Congress. Disappointed at her failure to get dominion status, India now demanded full independence.

The whole country was excited. Everybody was waiting for the lead from Gandhi. After two months of suspense, a Salt Satyagraha was announced by Gandhi.

This would be the beginning of a civil disobedience campaign in which laws made by the State would be broken. Civil disobedience would begin by breaking the salt law.

"Salt suddenly became a mysterious word, a word of power," Nehru said.

The government had put an excise tax on salt which brought an enormous amount of money to the treasury. Moreover, the government had the monopoly of manufacturing salt.

With Sarojini Naidu on the march to Dandi, 1930

The salt tax was to be attacked and the salt laws were to be broken. The very simplicity of Gandhi's choice made the issue more dramatic.

On March 2, 1930, Gandhi wrote a letter to the new Viceroy, Lord Irwin, about the deplorable condition of India under the British rule.

"The British rule," he said, "has impoverished the dumb millions by a system of progressive exploitation, and by a ruinously expensive military and civil administration which the country can never afford. It has reduced us politically to serfdom. It has sapped the foundations of our culture..."

He requested the Viceroy to see him and discuss the matter with him in person. "But if you cannot see your way to deal with these evils," he went on, "and my letter makes no appeal to your heart, on the eleventh day of this month I shall proceed, with such co-workers of the ashram as I can take, to disregard the provisions of the salt laws... It is, I know, open to you to frustrate my design by arresting me. I hope there will be tens of thousands ready, in a disciplined manner, to take up the work after me..."

Lord Irwin did not answer Gandhi but sent a message through his secretary expressing regret that Gandhi had chosen a course which involved breaking the law of the

The march to Dandi, 1930

land and which would be a danger to public peace.

The whole of India was agitated over Gandhi's Salt Satyagraha. On March 12, at 6.30 in the morning, thousands of people watched as Gandhi started from his ashram with 78 volunteers on a march to Dandi, a village on the sea coast 241 miles away.

There, it was announced, the salt law would be broken. Gandhi led the march from village to village, stopping at each place to talk to the peasants and to advise them on the necessity of social reforms.

For 24 days the eyes of India and the world followed Gandhi as he marched towards the sea. The government did not take the risk of arresting Gandhi. With each passing day the campaign grew. Hundreds and thousands of people joined the procession. Men, women, and children lined the route, offering flowers and shouting slogans for the victory of the march. Newspaper reporters from every corner of the world were there to report the progress of Gandhi's march.

The march ended on April 5 at Dandi village. Gandhi and his selected followers went to the sea-shore and broke the salt law by picking up salt left on the shore by the sea.

Gandhi then gave a signal to all Indians to manufacture salt illegally. He wanted the people to break the salt law openly and to prepare themselves for non-violent resistance to police action.

All over India people swarmed to the nearest sea coast to break the salt law. Only a few people knew how to make salt, but the people soon found their own ways of making it. All that mattered was the breaking of the salt law.

Gandhi and other leaders had made arrangements for the continuation of the agitation if they were arrested. A chain of leaders had been chosen so that, as each leader was arrested, another would be ready to take his place.

The government waited for some time before taking any  action, and then at last retaliation began. Gandhi was left at liberty, but many other leaders were taken into custody. Jawaharlal, Mahadev Desai (Gandhi's secretary) and Gandhi's son, Devadas, were the first to be sent to jail. In dealing with the breakers of the salt law, the police resorted to their usual brutal methods.

The Indian National

Picking up salt to break the law

94

Congress was declared illegal. Some newspapers which were threatened with censorship suspended publication. The people held hartals and demonstrations and mass arrests were made. Soon the jails were overcrowded with people who remained non-violent, lest Gandhi should call off the movement.

Gandhi then informed the Viceroy that he was going to raid the government-run Dharasana Salt Works in Gujarat.

Lord Irwin decided to act. Two English officers with pistols, accompanied by many Indian policemen armed with rifles, arrived at Gandhi's camp in the middle of the night.

They woke up Gandhi and said, "You are under arrest."

Gandhi was taken to Yerawada Central Jail.

So Gandhi was not there at the time of raid on the Dharasana Salt Works.

The salt deposits were surrounded by barbed-wire fencing and protected by about 400 Indian policemen armed with steel-shod lathis. A few British officers were in command of them.

Gandhi's volunteers halted some distance away from the fencing. Then a selected group of them advanced towards the barbed-wire fence. Police officials ordered the volunteers to disperse but they ignored the warning.

Suddenly the police rushed at them and rained blow after blow on the defenceless men. Not one of the volunteers even raised an arm to stop the blows. They fell down, some with broken skulls, some with broken shoulders, arms, or legs. The waiting crowd groaned.

When the entire first batch had been knocked down and carried off on stretchers, another batch advanced to meet the same fate. The campaign went on for hours. Finally, as the heat of the day increased, the volunteers stopped their

In many parts of India people broke the salt law.

activities for that day. Among the volunteers two had died and 320 were injured.

Gandhi's arrest had created a great sensation in India and abroad. Representations were sent from all parts of the world to the British Prime Minister asking the government to release Gandhi and make peace with India.

Even those who were supporters of the British demanded the release of Gandhi.

Gandhi proved to be more dangerous inside the jail than outside. While he sat quietly in Yerawada Jail, countrywide outbreaks of civil disobedience were greatly taxing the British. The jails were filled to overflowing. The government was in distress and finally, in 1931, they released Gandhi, Nehru and other leaders.

As soon as Gandhi was out of prison he asked for an interview with the Viceroy, Lord Irwin. The interview was immediately given. Gandhi and Irwin met, but the two men seemed to have come from two different worlds.

Gandhi did not go to seek any favours. He wanted to negotiate on terms of equality. The meeting went on for many days and finally the talks culminated in a treaty, the

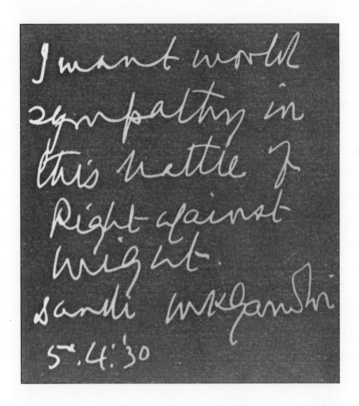

I want world sympathy in this battle of Right against Might.

Sardi M.K.Gandhi

5th.4.'30

Gandhi-Irwin Pact. It embodied compromises made by both sides. Irwin agreed to release all the political prisoners, and Gandhi promised to suspend civil disobedience and send a Congress representative to the Round Table Conference. For at that time, in London, the British Government was holding a Round Table Conference on the future of India.

The Gandhi-Irwin Pact was a victory for non-violent resistance. But some of Gandhi's Congress followers thought he had not gained much as a result of the pact.

Gandhi was designated as the sole representative of the Congress to the Round Table Conference. In August 1931 he sailed for London with a small party.

Gandhi went to England with the object of reaching an agreement with the British on a fair Constitution for India and also of winning the hearts of the British people. In his first object he failed, but in the second he met with great success. Gandhi spent 84 days in England and most of the time he was meeting and talking to people. Winston Churchill refused to see him but Gandhi captivated the hearts of many. He had tea with the King and Queen. When a reporter asked him if he thought he had been dressed well enough for such an august tea party, Gandhi replied, "The King had on enough for both of us."

At the Round Table Conference nothing was conceded to India towards her goal of Swaraj. The Conference played up the differences between Hindus and Muslims, and this only served to worsen communal tension in India.

Gandhi returned with nothing except warm goodwill for India from the hearts of many English people.

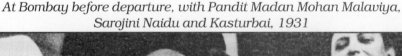

At Bombay before departure, with Pandit Madan Mohan Malaviya, Sarojini Naidu and Kasturbai, 1931

*With Sarojini Naidu, Mirabehn and other leaders on
the deck of* S.S. RAJPUTANA, *1931*

*At the second Round Table Conference (London); Pandit Madan Mohan
Malaviya, Srinivasa Shastri and Tej Bahadur Sapru on Gandhi's left, 1931*

At Marseilles, with C.F. Andrews, Muriel Lester, Mahadev Desai,
Mirabehn, and Pyarelal, 1931

With women workers in a Lancashire cotton mill, 1931

21

At home Gandhi found that the government had returned to the policy of repression. There were widespread arrests and the government seized the properties and bank balances of people and organizations who were hostile to their interests.

Early in 1932 Gandhi wanted to meet the new Viceroy, Lord Willingdon, but the Viceroy made it clear that the days of negotiation were over.

Gandhi informed the authorities that he was again starting a civil disobedience campaign. The Viceroy thought it was a threat. He had Gandhi arrested and imprisoned in Yerawada Central Jail. Several other leaders and many of Gandhi's followers were also arrested and sent to jail.

In March the struggle entered a new phase. Gandhi had always insisted that the untouchables were a part of the Hindus and must be treated as Hindus. Now, however, it was announced that the British proposed to set up separate voting for the untouchables. That meant that untouchables could vote only for members of their own caste.

Gandhi regarded the Hindu religion as one and

indivisible. He saw the game the British were playing. It was an attempt to weaken Hindu society.

"Separate treatment of untouchables cannot be allowed," declared Gandhi. "Here is an attempt to make untouchability last forever. Unless untouchability is destroyed we can never have self-government."

"But what can you do about it now?" asked a friend.

"I will resist this evil provision with my life," said Gandhi.

Gandhi announced that he would soon start a fast unto death unless the plan for separate electorates was changed.

The public announcement of his intention threw the country into panic. The Indian leaders were shocked at Gandhi's decision. Even Jawaharlal Nehru thought that he was taking a drastic step on a side issue.

During the time between the announcement and the day when Gandhi's fast was to begin, streams of visitors arrived at Yerawada Jail. The authorities, anxious to avoid any tragedy, allowed everyone to have free access to Gandhi. But all efforts to dissuade Gandhi from fasting were of no avail. The die was cast. Gandhi would fast.

Tagore sent him a telegram: "It is worth sacrificing precious life for the sake of India's unity and her social integrity. Our sorrowing hearts will follow your sublime penance with reverence and love."

Gandhi started his fast on September 20, 1932. The first day of the fast was observed all over India as a day of prayer and fasting. Many temples were opened to untouchables and meetings were held all over India urging the removal of untouchability.

Outside the jail political activity boiled. Leaders of caste Hindus and untouchables met and discussed various measures to arrive at a compromise that would satisfy

Gandhi. Proposals and counter-proposals were made and rejected. Dr. Bhim Rao Ambedkar, the most powerful leader of the untouchables, met Gandhi and assured him that he would try his best to find a solution.

A mud hut in Sevagram which Gandhi founded in 1940

On the third day of his fast, Gandhi's condition became bad. He grew very weak and he had to be carried to the bathroom on a stretcher. His blood pressure started rising. The authorities panicked and sent for his wife. They also allowed all his friends and followers to be with him.

The Indian people felt desperate. Gandhi might die and leave them leaderless. The other political leaders had failed, for they were unable to find a solution which would enable Gandhi to break his fast.

But on the fifth day of the fast the caste Hindu and untouchable leaders finally reached an agreement and signed a pact that would do away with separate electorates.

Gandhi, however, would not accept this unless it had been ratified by the British.

The news came that the British had approved of the pact; but still Gandhi would not break his fast until he saw the text of the approval.

One day, Tagore paid him a visit. The poet was so moved by Gandhi's condition that he put his head on Gandhi's chest and wept.

The text of the British approval came. Gandhi

accepted it and the epic fast was at last over.

Gandhi was released from prison in 1933. Shortly afterwards he suspended the mass civil disobedience movement, but sanctioned individual civil resistance to the government's brutal policy.

For the next seven years, Gandhi worked hard for the social and spiritual progress of his people. Many leaders, including Nehru, did not approve of Gandhi's policy.

"But," Nehru said, "how can I even think of advising a magician?" The 'magician' continued to win Nehru's unstinted devotion.

Sabarmati Ashram had been seized by the government during the Salt Satyagraha, so Gandhi now established a little retreat at Sevagram near Wardha in Maharashtra. This became his headquarters.

New reforms sponsored by the government got little support from the people of India. However, many people, including Congressmen, wanted to try them out as a means of furthering the cause of Swaraj.

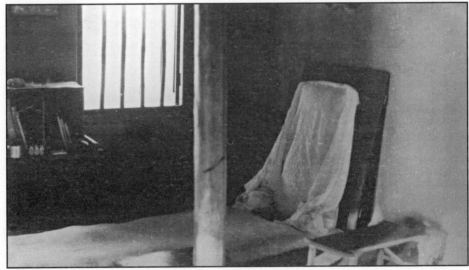

Gandhi's room at Sevagram

22

In 1939 the Second World War broke out. England and France declared war on Nazi Germany. Without consulting Indian leaders, Britain declared India to be at war on the allies' side.

Gandhi's sympathies were with the British, but he believed that all violence was evil and he would, therefore, have nothing to do with the war effort, although he gave England his moral support.

The Indian National Congress wanted to help Britain and fight on the allies' side, but only as a free nation. But to grant India independence seemed ridiculous to Churchill and his government. They had no intention of letting India go by default. Britain refused to accept the cooperation offered by the Congress.

As a protest, all the Congress ministries in the provinces resigned. The government took over the administration and they acted in such a way as to help their war effort. Acting on the goodwill and restraint taught by Gandhi, the Indian leaders showed no reaction.

Events in Europe were having repercussions in India,

With the president of the Haripura Congress, Subhas Chandra Bose, 1938

however. The Congress Working Committee found itself unable to accept in its entirety Gandhi's attitude to the war. In particular they would not accept his view that the defence of India should not depend on armed force.

The leaders met again and again in Gandhi's room at Sevagram and talked of their desire to start some action. Finally, a proposal was put forward that all provincial governments should join with the British authorities in the defence of India. The government, however, rejected the offer.

In September 1940, a meeting of the All-India Congress Committee was held in Bombay. There, as a protest against England's utter indifference to India's hopes, it was decided to launch individual civil disobedience against the authorities. It was also decided to hold meetings to protest against British imperialism. At that time such meetings were forbidden.

Vinobha Bhave was the first to inaugurate individual satyagraha. He was arrested and so were hundreds of others who followed him. Nehru also was arrested. Within a few months over 30,000 Congressmen were put in jail.

Gandhi alone was not imprisoned. He devoted his time

to spreading the gospel of truth and non-violence. In December 1941 the government released all the satyagrahis. Then, in 1942, as the Japanese swept across the Pacific and went through Malaya and Burma (now Myanmar), the British began to think of a settlement with India. Japan might even invade India.

With the threat of invasion by Japan even Gandhi began to feel that his pacifism might stand in the way of India's future. So he made the proposal of a provisional government so that all the resources of India could be added to the government's side in the struggle against the aggressors. But this proposal was ignored.

In March 1942 Churchill announced that the war cabinet had agreed on a plan for India and that Sir Stafford Cripps had agreed to go to India to find out whether the Indian leaders would accept the plan, and whether they would devote all their thought and energy to the defence of India against Japan.

With Tagore at Santiniketan, 1940

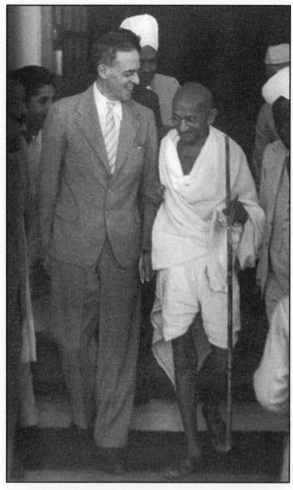

With Sir Stafford Cripps in Delhi, 1942

Sir Stafford Cripps arrived in Delhi on March 22. He met Gandhi, Nehru, Azad, Jinnah and other important leaders. Cripps promised greater freedom than that which had been offered before. He also offered complete freedom after the war if India wanted it. The leaders would perhaps have accepted this offer if it had come a year earlier, but now they rejected it.

The Congress leaders did not want any compromise based on promises. The British did not trust the people of India sufficiently to give them any real power, and so the Indian leaders felt that they could not trust the British to hand over power after the war.

23

In August 1942 the All-India Congress Committee met in Bombay and was presided over by Maulana Abul Kalam Azad. Again the demand to set up a provisional government was made.

"We can no longer hold back our people from exercising their will," Gandhi said. "Nor can we go on eternally submitting to the imperialist policy. The time has come for the English to go. Civil servants, army officers, government officers all of them should quit India."

The 'Quit India' resolution was drawn up and passed by the meeting for presentation to the government. Jawaharlal moved the resolution and Sardar Patel seconded it.

The resolution also announced the starting of a mass struggle on the widest possible scale.

Winding up the meeting Gandhi said, "I have pledged the Congress, and the Congress has pledged herself that she will do or die."

The government did not wait for the mass movement to begin. Overnight Gandhi was arrested, and also many other leaders in various parts of India. Gandhi was interned in the Aga Khan Palace in Poona. Mahadev Desai, Kasturbai, Sarojini Naidu and Mirabehn were also taken there.

But with the leaders in jail, India did not remain idle. 'Do or die' was taken up by the people. There were mass movements everywhere. And there was a great outburst of violence throughout the country. People started destroying government buildings and whatever else they considered to be symbols of British imperialism.

Shortly after his detention in the Aga Khan Palace, Gandhi suffered a grievous bereavement. Mahadev Desai, his faithful and able secretary, died of a heart attack.

"Mahadev has lived up to the 'do or die' mantra," Gandhi said. "His sacrifice cannot but hasten the day of India's deliverance."

All over India there were strikes and disorder. Lord Linlithgow, the Viceroy, attributed all this to Gandhi. Gandhi had invited violence, he claimed. In a long series of letters to Lord Linlithgow, Gandhi tried to persuade him to retract this charge against him.

Failing in this, Gandhi decided to undertake a fast as "an appeal to the Highest Tribunal" against the unjust charges. Gandhi fasted for 21 days in February 1943. It was a great ordeal, but he survived the fast.

Kasturbai nursed him back to health, but her own health was failing. She suffered two heart attacks. Gandhi tried his best to save her, but Kasturbai's condition grew worse. One day she died quietly in Gandhi's arms.

A few weeks later Gandhi was taken seriously ill with malaria. The Indian people demanded his immediate release and the authorities, believing that he was nearing death, released him. Gandhi was slowly restored to health.

The demand for Indian Independence had now grown

into a world-wide question. Apart from India's own attitude, America and other countries pressed Britain to grant freedom to India. Churchill did not yield to any of these approaches. India had always been of help to British prosperity and Churchill was the last man to think of giving up India and thus make Britain the poorer.

Two months after Germany's surrender in May 1945, the Labour Party came into power in Britain and Clement Attlee became the Prime Minister. After the defeat of Japan a few months later, the British Government announced that they expected to grant self-government to India as soon as her internal problems could be solved.

This was a victory for India. It was a victory for non-violence. Britain, defeated by the peaceful revolution, could not hold on to India any longer. Britain agreed to a planned withdrawal from India, without bitterness and in friendship.

All through his life Gandhi had worked for unity between

With Muhammad Ali Jinnah Bombay, 1944

the Hindus and the Muslims. But he had not had much success. There was a large section of nationalist Muslims in the Congress, but the heads of the Muslim League were drifting further and further away.

Gandhi was not the man to give up hope, however, and he pursued his efforts to bring about a settlement. On the other hand, Muhammad Ali Jinnah, the leader of the Muslim League, was hostile to the idea of unity. He demanded a separate Muslim State before freedom was given to India.

The Viceroy invited all the leaders to Simla (now Shimla) and tried to find a solution and bring about Hindu-Muslim unity. However, Jinnah insisted on having a separate State, to be called Pakistan.

With Lord Pethick Lawrence, 1946

Britain announced an election in India which was held. The Congress won most of the non-Muslim seats and the Muslim League won most of the Muslim seats. The deadlock continued.

"We can settle the problem in ten minutes if Mr. Gandhi agrees to the creation of Pakistan," said Jinnah.

"Cut me in two," cried Gandhi, but do not cut India in two."

He spoke to deaf ears.

In February 1946 the British Government sent a Cabinet Mission to India. It consisted of Lord Pethick Lawrence, Sir Stafford Cripps, and A.V. Alexander. The task of the Cabinet Mission was to study the situation and suggest what should be done. After careful consideration the Cabinet Mission issued a statement proposing the withdrawal of British authority from India. They had the idea of a united India.

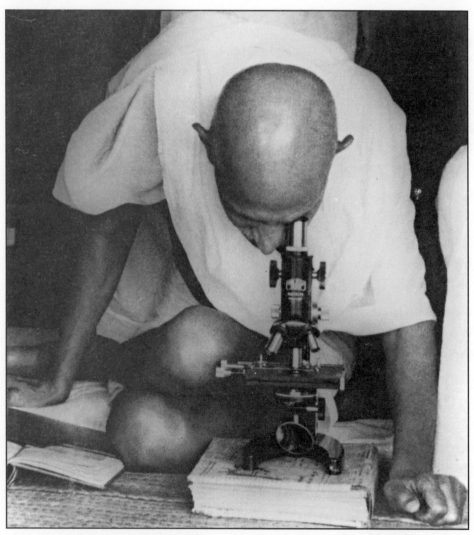

Studying the leprosy germs with a microscope, Seagon 1939

24

On August 24, the Viceroy announced the formation of an Interim National Government to replace the Viceroy's Executive Council.

Jawaharlal Nehru was the Vice-President of the Interim Government.

The Muslim League declined to join it on the ground that it had not been given the right to nominate all the Muslim members.

After the installation of the Interim Government, Gandhi was anxious to return to Sevagram, his ashram near Wardha, but the Congress leaders prevailed on him to stay longer in Delhi because they wanted his advice. So Gandhi stayed on in Delhi.

Then the Muslim League decided to join the Interim Government and an announcement was made to this effect on October 15, 1946. Gandhi once again felt free to return to Sevagram. He was about to leave Delhi when news came of the disturbances in Bengal. There was widespread communal rioting by the Muslims in Calcutta and in the Muslim majority district of Noakhali in East

With his peace mission on his way to riot-affected villages, Noakhali, 1946

Bengal, with murder, arson, looting, forced conversions, forced marriages and abduction.

Gandhi was confused and grief-stricken. Instead of returning to Sevagram, he set out for Noakhali to try to bring peace there.

The communal riots spread. There were similar riots in Bihar and the Punjab. Thousands were killed and thousands more were injured. Gandhi was greatly disheartened by these events. He tried to calm and reassure the people.

He walked from village to village and from house to house carrying his message of peace. Wherever he was, there was peace, at least outwardly. But the general situation in India was worsening. Rioting spread from the towns to the villages. In Bihar the Muslims were suffering and Gandhi went there to instil courage into the Muslim minority and to help them in their distress.

The situation in India was so dreadful that the Congress leaders realized that the best way open to them was to accept Jinnah's demand for a division of the country, and they reluctantly approved the formation of Pakistan.

Nehru met Gandhi to inform him of this decision.

Gandhi asked him, "Is there no way out? No hope of a united India?"

Nehru was sad and grave.

"Bapuji," he replied, "unity is impossible. Dreadful as is the idea of a separate country within our borders, we have to accept it. Otherwise this deadly turmoil will never cease."

Gandhi bowed his head to hide his despair.

On June 3, 1947, Attlee, the British Prime Minister, announced the plan for partition. The Congress and the Muslim League accepted it.

With Lord and Lady Mountbatten

For Gandhi it was a spiritual tragedy. With infinite sadness he said, "All India must accept Pakistan in loving resignation. We have no choice. Hindus must lead the way to a friendly settlement."

Lord Mountbatten, the last British Viceroy, was anxious not to delay the ushering in of Independent India and Independent Pakistan. He shortened the time limit for the British to

116

quit India. The date for the declaration of Indian Independence was fixed for August 15, 1947.

On that day, India's long struggle and suffering for freedom was over. A new nation, although split in two, was born.

Lord Mountbatten hailed Gandhi as 'the architect of India's freedom through non-violence'.

Gandhi had never given his approval to partition, but when it was done he accepted it and did everything possible for the attainment of Hindu-Muslim friendship. Yet the tension between Hindus and Muslims was on the rise.

As a result of partition over 7,00,000 Hindus, Sikhs, and other non-Muslims in Pakistan, fearing the Muslims, left their homes and set out towards India. From India about the same number of Muslims, fearing the Hindus, left their homes for Pakistan. The miseries attendant on this mass migration, one of the greatest in history, were manifold. Over 1,50,000 people on the move were exposed to starvation, disease and massacre on the way.

Gandhi was on his way to the Punjab when he stopped in Delhi, hoping to quell the riots that had broken out there. He was very distressed at the inhuman way the Delhi Hindus were treating the Muslims.

Gandhi's gospel of forbearance and forgiveness towards Muslims marked him as a traitor in the eyes of many Hindu extremists. In the face of fanatical opposition, Gandhi redoubled his efforts and the major disturbances in Delhi subsided, but there were still troubles here and there.

Gandhi decided to do penance by fasting, which he thought would bring about a change in the attitude of the Hindu fanatics.

The fast began on January 13, 1948. There was gloom all over India at the news of Gandhi's fast.

Walking to the prayer meeting at Birla House, New Delhi on January 29, 1948

People thought that he would not be able to survive another fast. The whole world watched as 78-year-old Gandhi fasted to save his country from destruction.

On January 18 a peace committee, representing all communities, met and signed a pact pledging unity and the protection of life, property and faith to the Muslim minority.

Gandhi was informed of the pledge and he broke his fast.

Gandhi was staying at Birla House. Every evening he held a prayer meeting in the grounds.

During his prayer meeting on January 20, a bomb was thrown at him, but it missed its target. Gandhi continued his prayer meeting as if nothing had happened.

"Bapuji, a bomb exploded near you," said a voice.

"Really?" Gandhi said. "Perhaps some poor fanatic threw it. Let no one look down on him."

On January 30, after a midday nap, Gandhi woke up at 3.30 p.m. The whole day he had had a stream of visitors. Sardar Patel went to see him at 4 o'clock. Nehru and Azad were to come after the evening prayers.

Gandhi left his room at 5 o'clock and went towards the prayer meeting.

He passed through a cordoned-off path, accompanied by Manu and Abha, his granddaughters. As he was walking along, a youth came forward as if to seek his blessings. But he stood in front of Gandhi and at point-blank range fired three shots in quick succession. All the bullets hit him.

Gandhi fell, uttering the prayer, "Rama! Rama!"

Gandhi was dead.

The assassination gave the world a tremendous shock.

Nehru told the country of Gandhi's death, his voice choked with emotion:

"Friends and comrades, the light has gone out of our lives and there is darkness everywhere. I do not know what to tell you and how to say it. Our beloved leader, Bapu as we called him, the Father of the Nation, is no more. Perhaps I am wrong to say that. Nevertheless, we will not see him again as we have seen him for these many years...

"The light has gone out, I said, and yet I was wrong. For the light that shone in this country was no ordinary light.

The light that has illumined this country for these many years will illumine this country for many more years, and a thousand years later that light will still be seen in this country, and the world will see it and it will give solace to innumerable hearts..."

The funeral procession of Mahatma Gandhi on way to Rajghat, New Delhi, January 31, 1948